Minimal Rationality

Computational Models of Cognition and Perception

Editors

Jerome A. Feldman
Patrick J. Hayes
David E. Rumelhart

Minimal Rationality

Christopher Cherniak

A Bradford Book
The MIT Press
Cambridge, Massachusetts
London, England

This book was set in Baskerville by Achorn Graphic Services, Inc., and printed and bound by Halliday Lithograph in the United States of America.

Library of Congress Cataloging-in-Publication Data

Cherniak, Christopher.
  Minimal rationality.

  "A Bradford book."
  (Computational models of cognition and perception)
  Contains selections presented as author's thesis
(Ph. D.)—University of California, Berkeley, 1977)
under title: Beliefs and logical abilities.
  Bibliography: p.
  Includes index.
  1. Reasoning. 2. Knowledge, Theory of.
I. Title. II. Series.
BC177.C52   1986   121   86-7497
  ISBN 0-262-03122-1

For S. G. C., G. S. C., and G. C. C.

Contents

II
EPISTEMOLOGICAL IMPLICATIONS

4
The "Universal Acceptance of Logic"   75

5
The Special Reasons Requirement   100

6
Limits for Knowledge   122

Preface

The basic idea behind this project came to me nearly two decades ago when I first encountered C. S. Peirce's definition of
truth in terms of inquiry pursued to an ideal limit. I wondered
whether there would be truths, and inferential tasks, too
"large" in some philosophically interesting sense for human
beings—or any feasible creature—to manage. Thus began my
exploration of the thesis that agents are finite objects, and my
pursuit of the White Whale of excessively idealized models of
the epistemic agent. I started to follow out the pervasive consequences of standard rationality idealizations for philosophy
and, more broadly, for what was to become known as the "cognitive sciences." And I attempted to construct more psychologically and computationally realistic models of the "minimal
agent."

This little book therefore has a long and rather untidy ancestry. Much of the most directly Peircean material, which was to
become chapter 6 of the present work, first appeared as my
B.Litt. thesis, "Pragmatism and Realism," at the University of
Oxford in 1973. The substance of what is chapters 1 through 4
here, with the exception of the discussion of computational
complexity theory, wound up as my Ph.D. dissertation, "Beliefs
and Logical Abilities," at the University of California, Berkeley,
in 1977. Instead of then directly attempting a book, I opted for
the strategy of first publishing a series of articles, each self-
contained, that introduced the elements of the program of developing a less idealized theory of rationality.

In this way, much of the material of chapter 1 was published,
in different form, as "Minimal Rationality," *Mind* 90 (1981);
chapter 2 as "Feasible Inferences," *Philosophy of Science* 48
(1981); chapter 3 as "Rationality and the Structure of Human
Memory," *Synthese* 57 (1983); chapter 4 as "Computational

Complexity and the Universal Acceptance of Logic," *Journal of Philosophy* 81 (1984); and chapter 6 as "Limits for Knowledge," *Philosophical Studies* 49 (1986). Chapter 5 consists of hitherto unpublished material. The present book provides an opportunity to present the entire argument for the first time, to work out interrelations among its main points; the previously published material has been revised, augmented, and somewhat rearranged here.

Some earlier incarnations of chapters 2, 3, and 4 were prepared with assistance from the Tufts University Faculty Research Grant Program, the American Philosophical Society, and the National Endowment for the Humanities, respectively. I am grateful for their moral, as well as fiscal, support. I am also happy to have received a University of Maryland General Research Board book subsidy award.

Many teachers and colleagues helped in many ways over the long history of this project. I am especially indebted to G. E. M. Anscombe, Lenore Blum, Charles Chihara, Herbert Clark, William Craig, Daniel Dennett, William Gutowski, Kathleen Hemenway, Dennis Hill, Richard Karp, David Pears, Eleanor Rosch, Jarrett Rosenberg, Michael Slote, Stephen Stich, Barry Stroud, Mark Tuttle, and Scott Weinstein. Others have affected the project in ways perhaps more indirect, but no less important; I particularly want to thank my old friends Peter Eggenberger, William G. Quinn, and Thomas Schaefer.

University of Maryland
October 1985

I

The Minimal Agent

1

Minimal Rationality

The most basic law of psychology is a rationality constraint on an agent's beliefs, desires, and actions: No rationality, no agent. How rational must a creature be to be an agent, that is, to qualify as having a cognitive system of beliefs, desires, perceptions? Until recently, philosophy has uncritically accepted highly idealized conceptions of rationality. But cognition, computation, and information have costs; they do not just subsist in some immaterial effluvium. We are, after all, only human.

There is a need to examine what can be characterized as the next most fundamental psychological principle: Agents are finite objects. In this chapter I will sketch a first approximation of a theory of a *minimal agent* who has fixed limits on cognitive resources such as time and memory. In particular, according to such a more realistic account, an agent can have a less than perfect deductive ability. I will argue that, although in everyday psychological explanations of behavior we require rationality of an agent, we in fact require only minimal, as distinguished from ideal, rationality. I will further propose that such minimal rationality conditions are indispensable for adequate cognitive theory. What is at stake concerns the very possibility of a cognitive science and of a realist interpretation of it.

1.1 The "Autonomy of the Mental"

In "A Scandal in Bohemia" Sherlock Holmes's opponent has hidden a very important photograph in a room, and Holmes wants to find out where it is. Holmes has Watson throw a smoke bomb into the room and yell "Fire!" when Holmes's opponent is in the next room, while Holmes watches. Then, as one would expect, the opponent runs into the room and takes the photograph from its hiding place. Not everyone would have devised such an ingenious plan for manipulating an opponent's behavior; but once the conditions are described, it seems very easy to predict the opponent's actions. Prima facie, we predict the actions not as commonsense behaviorists or neurophysiologists, but by assuming that the opponent possesses a large set of beliefs and desires—including the desire to preserve the photograph, and belief that where there's smoke there's fire, the belief that fire will destroy the photograph, and so on—and that the opponent will act appropriately for those beliefs and desires.

It seems an uncontroversial fact that we very commonly employ this procedure for predicting people's behavior in everyday situations. A less exotic case than the Holmes story is that often when I step onto a crosswalk, I am betting my life (not always with complete equanimity) on expectations of a motorist's behavior that seem based on assumptions regarding his perceptions, beliefs, and desires. Other people and their actions are very important to us; much of the framework of our commonsense cognitive theory is probably innate, refined by natural selection.

The idea that there can be a predictive theory of belief is of course not new (see, for example, the review in Hempel 1965, sec. 10). However, a long-standing and central tradition in the philosophy of mind denies the possibility, even in principle, of such predictions of behavior on the basis of attribution of a cognitive system. Descartes's distinction between the domains of the physical and the mental (for example, 1955c), where the former is subject to deterministic laws while the latter is free, has such a consequence. This type of view continues to be significant in the current debate concerning the possibility and nature of cognitive psychology. For example, Donald Davidson defends a quasi-autonomist position by arguing that there can be "strict" or "serious" deterministic laws only in the physical domain and that psychological theories cannot yield "accurate" predictions (1980a,b,c). I think the influence of the view can also be perceived in D. C. Dennett's paper "Intentional Systems" (1978a). At the beginning of the paper Dennett proposes to examine the concept of "a system whose behavior can be (at least sometimes) explained and predicted by relying on ascriptions to the system of beliefs and desires" (p. 3). And yet there is a tension; by the end of the paper Dennett is claiming, "If one wants to predict and explain the 'actual, empirical' behavior of believers, one must . . . cease talking of belief and descend to the design stance or physical stance for one's account" (p. 22).

There is some conflict between the simple fact of the success of commonsense psychological practice and philosophical assertions of the autonomy of the mental, even when that autonomy is attenuated to a matter of degree of precision of laws. This chapter examines one source of this conflict. I will not attempt to disprove every one of the burgeoning multitude of arguments for the impossibility of a predictive cognitive theory; I will argue only that one crucial precondition for a cognitive theory with predictive content has been mistakenly rejected by a number of these positions. The main hypothesis here is that the pervasively and tacitly assumed conception of rationality in philosophy is so idealized that it cannot apply in an interesting way to actual human beings. One significant consequence of such an extreme idealization is that it tends to exclude a realist account of mental entities in favor of an instrumentalist account, such as Dennett's: if the only possible rationality conditions on cognitive systems are so idealized as to be inapplicable to human beings, then any attributions of such systems to human beings cannot really be *true*; the attributed entities are at most useful myths.

I will be exploring the implications of a concept of minimal rationality, where the agent has a less than perfect ability to choose appropriate actions. I will be principally concerned with rationality conditions on belief sets and on the believer's deductive abilities. These will only be necessary conditions on agenthood. One major reason why they cannot be sufficient is that they are only forward-looking, to actions caused by beliefs. The conditions below do not deal with the upstream informational origin of beliefs; I will not address questions of why and how beliefs represent the world. The strategy in approaching the question of what minimal rationality is will be to proceed by successive approximations.

1.2 Two Types of Belief Theory

Rationality conditions can be either too weak or too strong for a satisfactory predictive theory. Before we consider theories of belief that presuppose ideal rationality, let us examine the opposite type of theory, one that requires no rationality at all of an agent *A*. The most rudimentary theory of this kind is an *assent theory of belief*:

A believes all and only those statements that *A* would affirm.

Russell's theory of belief in "On Propositions" included an internalized version of this public assent criterion of belief.[1] According to Russell, a person believes a proposition at a particular time when the believed proposition occurs with a "feeling of assent" to the proposition in the person's psychological history at the time. (This basic idea might also seem to underlie Davidson's (1984b) "no language, no thought" position; but in fact Davidson arrives at a decision-theoretic inspired idealization of the type discussed later in this section.)

Such a theory has an attractive simplicity and perhaps tends to satisfy feelings that a believer is the final authority on what his beliefs are. However, a crucial defect of the assent theory as a complete theory is that it does not impose any rationality constraints upon the belief set, or more than vestigial constraints upon the relation of the belief-desire set to the agent's actions. It is a "null" rationality requirement. According to the assent theory, no inferences, however obvious and useful, need be made from the beliefs, and the belief set can include any and all inconsistencies. The belief-desire set is not required to guide at all the choice of appropriate actions, except for the small area of verbal behavior of assent and dissent; this is a lethal impoverishment of the evidence base for belief attribution. Consequently, the assent theory does entail the autonomy of the mental, and it makes a mystery of our everyday successes in predicting behavior on the basis of belief-desire attributions.

A cognitive theory with no rationality restrictions is without predictive content; using it, we can have virtually no expectations regarding a believer's behavior. There is also a further metaphysical, as opposed to epistemological, point concerning rationality as part of what it is to be a *person*: the elements of a mind—and, in particular, a cognitive system—must *fit together* or cohere. A collection of mynah bird utterances or snippets of the *New York Times* are chaos, and so (at most) just a sentence set, not a belief set. Again, no rationality, no agent. (This point seems worth keeping in mind when one is considering the natural impulse to outflank, or outdo, the minimalist position of this book by denying that there are *any* absolute rationality constraints.)

In contrast to the permissiveness of the assent theory, the most prevalent accounts of belief have included conditions requiring ideal rationality of an agent. In economic, decision, and game theory the principle that the agent will generally choose (or is likely to choose) the action that maximizes his expected utility is commonly recognized as being of this type. Although this principle does have valuable applicability for certain ranges of problems, some realization has begun to emerge in decision and economic theory and psychology relatively recently of the serious difficulties for models assuming perfect information or rationality of an agent as an idealization.[2] But in philosophy of psychology and mind and in the theory of knowledge this point has received particularly little attention. The philosophical accounts employ, usually tacitly, an *ideal general rationality condition*, which can be formulated roughly as

If *A* has a particular belief-desire set, *A* would undertake *all* and only actions that are apparently appropriate.

As a convenient simplification here, we will say that an action is *apparently appropriate* if and only if, according to *A*'s beliefs, it would tend to satisfy *A*'s desires. (A weaker ideal rationality condition is '*A* would undertake some nonempty set of apparently *most* appropriate actions'.)

Such an idealized theory of belief is of value as a convenient simplification of the theory we actually employ in everyday situations, but it is unacceptably stringent in important ways; for in fact this rationality condition is generally unrealizable. Of course, strictly applied, it would exclude the possibility of someone's having beliefs and desires and even occasionally being forgetful or careless in his choice of actions. But it is a platitude to point out that nobody is perfect, to err is human, and so on. Consequently, with only such a theory, Holmes could not have predicted his inevitably suboptimal opponent's behavior on the basis of an attribution of a belief-desire set; he could not have expected that her performance would fall short of rational perfection in any way, much less in any *particular* ways. Holmes would have to regard his opponent as not having a cognitive system. And the existence of suboptimal rationality seems more than mere trivial exceptions to the ideal rationality model. Consider the utility of the familiar "bloodshot eyes" strategy in our daily game-theoretic confrontations—the tactic of deliberately leading the opponent to believe one is incapable of evaluating costs of actions in a way that will maximize one's own position, so that the opponent will not even attempt various strategic manipulations.

But as I will discuss below, the ideal rationality condition requires an agent not only not to be sloppy but to have a peculiarly idealized deductive ability. The most important unsatisfactoriness of the ideal general rationality condition arises from its denial of a fundamental feature of human existence, that human beings are in the *finitary predicament* of having fixed limits on their cognitive capacities and the time available to them. Unlike Turing machines, actual human beings in everyday situations or even in scientific inquiry do not have potentially infinite memory and computing time. This is the "cognitive friction" the idealizations overlook. Since any human being is in the finitary predicament, using a cognitive theory with the ideal rationality condition seems to amount to having very nearly no applicable theory at all. Furthermore, the basic limitations imposed by the finitary predicament are not confined to creatures of our particular intellectual abilities. The limitations are general in that they would be just as unavoidable, for example, for a creature that had available the resources of the entire galaxy until heat-death of the universe. Thus, any assumption that the ideal general rationality condition is harmless, in that human rationality approximates it in most ways that are of interest, must be closely examined.

1.3 A Third Theory: Minimal Rationality

The value of an idealization is always relative to a set of goals. The ideal general rationality conditions is useful under some conditions, as Von Neumann and Morgenstern, for instance, explained for their game-theoretic models in *The Theory of Games and Economic Behavior* (1944). A sound motivation for idealizing a theory is that the resulting simplification yields a theory that is more manageable (for instance, for purposes of formalization) than an entirely correct or complete theory would be. A theory can be idealized to different degrees; simplicity and manageability can be traded off for greater applicability. In this way, there should be latitude for mutual coexistence among various idealizations. A minimal rationality theory attempts to navigate between Scylla and Charybdis, obtaining some significant applicability in exchange for a somewhat more complex theory. This rationality theory continues to be significantly idealized in the conception of inference. The account to follow will be principally concerned with verbally formulated beliefs. I will generally be treating an agent's beliefs as a set of sentences, and an inference from those beliefs as the addition of a sentence to that set. I will also not distinguish between deliberate, conscious inference and unconscious inference. All of the other minimal rationality conditions below can be derived from a *minimal general rationality condition*:

If *A* has a particular belief-desire set, *A* would undertake some, but not necessarily all, of those actions that are apparently appropriate.

The argument that as belief-attributers we in fact employ—and, in addition, *should* employ—this minimal condition is by exhaustion of a trichotomy. We have seen that we are able to predict people's behavior on the basis of belief-desire attributions and that both ideal and null rationality conditions largely exclude this. For we know that (1) no creature in the finitary predicament can satisfy the ideal rationality condition. And (2) if the agent were not required to be at least more likely to undertake some of the apparently appropriate actions, then a belief-desire set attribution could never yield any behavior predictions and would never be disconfirmable by observed behavior; on the basis of such an attribution, no behavior could be expected, and every action would be equally probable. (As mentioned, there is also the fact that believing *p* just *is*, among other things, being disposed to act appropriately (sometimes) for *p*.) In fact, recognition that some rationality condition on beliefs is required, combined with failure to distinguish minimal from ideal rationality, gives ideal rationality conditions a kind of "all or nothing" plausibility. Hence, (3) the only remaining possibility is "Moderation in all things, including rationality": a minimal rationality condition is what we must be using, and should use.

In addition, for a predictive cognitive theory, there is a stronger general rationality condition on an agent's belief-desire set. The agent must not only attempt some of the actions that are appropriate given the belief-desire set; he must also *not* attempt enough of the actions that are *in*appropriate given that belief-desire set (consequently, similar requirements accompany the minimal and ideal inference conditions below). According to a minimal general rationality condition without this additional requirement of "negative rationality," a random guesser—a creature whose behavior is merely determined by coin-tosses—is very likely, given enough time, to qualify as having any arbitrary belief-desire set. Similarly, the minimal general rationality condition is stronger than a purely extensional requirement, in that it has counterfactual implications.

A minimal general rationality condition implies that an agent must have a minimal deductive ability. (I will discuss more fully in chapter 5 the question of whether satisfaction of the minimal general rationality condition requires nondeductive ability.) The *minimal inference condition* on deductive ability is

If *A* has a particular belief-desire set, *A* would make some, but not necessarily all, of the sound inferences from the belief set that are apparently appropriate.

These inferences need not involve verbally represented beliefs. For our purposes, the agent's undertaking an action appropriate for his beliefs and desires, where the beliefs and desires cause the action "in the right way," constitutes his concluding that the action is desirable;³ an entirely nonlinguistic creature like a young child can perform such inferences.

The minimal inference condition requires an agent to make some of the sound inferences that are apparently useful in selecting appropriate actions. If an agent did not satisfy at least the minimal inference condition, in that he would make no apparently appropriate inferences from his beliefs, he would not generally be able to recognize and undertake actions that were appropriate given those beliefs. For example, suppose the person's putative belief set included the beliefs 'If it rains, then the dam will break' and 'It is raining'. The person would not conclude that the dam will break, even if this conclusion would be obviously useful—for instance, when the person also believed he was below the dam and would be drowned if it broke, was not suicidal, and so on. Therefore, the person would not be able to undertake any appropriate action on the basis of his beliefs (as opposed to, for example, by whim) that depended on this information, such as fleeing. The putative agent's deficit of logical insight, and so of rational action, would exclude him from having beliefs according to the minimal general rationality condition.

We can in turn describe the logical ability required by the minimal inference condition in terms of two other requirements. The *minimal heuristic requirement* on which inferences the agent would attempt to make is

A would undertake some of the sound inferences from the belief set that would be apparently appropriate for A to make.

That is, the resulting inferences would, according to A's own beliefs, aid A in choosing other actions that would tend to satisfy A's desires. (Objective appropriateness is not a satisfactory demand here, since to regard the agent's beliefs as always correct would clearly be an unacceptably extreme idealization.) The agent must act as if he had made judgments of probable cost and value of information of the form 'According to my beliefs and desires, it would be useful for me now to know whether or not q is a consequence of my beliefs $\{r,s, \ldots\}$', where some of these judgments are correct. Thus, a heuristic imbecile—for example, one who just tries to deduce from p vacuous conjunctions $p \& p$, $(p \& p) \& p$, $((p \& p) \& p) \& p$, etc.—cannot have beliefs. Each inquiry, deductive or otherwise, has costs; the heuristic imbecile would squander its limited cognitive resources on such valueless inferences and would therefore be paralyzed for apparently appropriate inferences. Thus, for creatures with limited resources (such as time pressures), heuristic imbecility by itself entails complete logical incompetence.

The *minimal deducing requirement* is

A must succeed in performing some of the apparently appropriate sound inferences that A has undertaken.

In stating separate heuristic and deducing requirements, there is no implication that two genuinely distinct processes always have occurred when an inference is made. The heuristic and deducing requirements are interdependent, in that deducing ability (and also some nondeductive reasoning ability) is required in selecting appropriate deductive tasks, and heuristic ability may be required (for instance, to identify useful lemmas) in order to perform complex deductive tasks already undertaken. The actual heuristic procedure of selecting apparently useful deductive questions is usually nonconscious. And there is a point of diminishing returns, beyond which there are other, better uses of an agent's time than in perfecting the choice of deductive questions to consider—for example, identifying some of the actions that will only be beneficial if performed at that time.

When we regard inferences as one variety of actions, the minimal heuristic requirement is a special case of the minimal general rationality condition on actions. However, apparently useful inferences cannot be selected solely by means of actual practical inferences—conscious or nonconscious—or there will be a regress.[4] As a first step toward avoiding this problem, we can say that in many cases the agent does not actually decide to undertake the inference. Rather, actions of inferring must instead come to conform with desires and beliefs largely by means of fixed, nonintegrated, nonconscious mechanisms of selection or guidance that do not involve reasoning processes of any kind. These mechanisms may be acquired—for instance, as learned "cognitive styles"—or natural selection may have "designed" the agent so that, as an efficient organism, he undertakes particular inferences. (I will return to this in section 5.7.)

1.4 Ideal Deductive Ability

The minimal inference condition is only a necessary condition for agenthood. Is the minimal inference condition (with the additional "negative rationality" condition) a sufficient condition for being logically competent to be an agent? As a start toward determining whether satisfaction of this augmented minimal inference condition constitutes possession of *all* the logical ability required of an agent, we can argue against conditions that require an agent to have ideal deductive ability. Let us first examine what ideal deductive ability is supposed to be, since there is a family of distinct types of "ideal."

The simplest, and most extreme, idealization is that an agent's belief set is *deductively closed*:

A actually believes (or, infers, or can infer) all and only consequences of *A*'s beliefs.

This is the rationality idealization adopted in classical epistemic logic, notably Hintikka's *Knowledge and Belief* (1962). But in trying to satisfy this condition, an agent faces an infinite task. It is impossible for a person to infer and believe every one of the consequences of one belief, because there are too many, however they may be individuated. This set of consequences includes the infinite set of all valid sentences expressible in the agent's language. In addition, most of these consequences are such that it is impossible to believe a single one of them; that is because each is so complex that it could not be read in a lifetime, much less understood. Of course, any cognitive theory that includes the deductive closure condition cannot apply to human beings, or indeed to any other creature in the finitary predicament. Hintikka himself explains that his axiomatization can be applied to the actual world "only in so far as our world approximates one of the 'most knowledgeable of possible worlds,' . . . in which everybody follows the consequences of what he knows as far as they lead him" (p. 36). We can now add: not very far.

In fact, the deductive closure condition requires more deductive ability than is needed to satisfy even the ideal general rationality condition, or related conditions, such as a principle of maximization of utility; for the deductive closure condition requires an agent to infer all consequences of his beliefs, whether apparently useful for him or not. The logical ability needed for a creature to satisfy the ideal general rationality condition is described by an *ideal inference condition*:

If *A* has a particular belief-desire set, *A* would make all and only sound inferences from the belief set that are apparently appropriate.

For our purposes, the ideal inference condition is equivalent to the following *ideal heuristic* and *ideal deducing requirements,* respectively, which correspond to the minimal heuristic and deducing requirements above:

(i) *A* would select all and only those inferences to make from the beliefs that are apparently appropriate for *A* to make.

(ii) *A* would successfully perform all and only those inferences.

If a creature did not satisfy both of these conditions, there might be some actions that were apparently appropriate, but that the creature could not recognize to be appropriate because it lacked the logical ability needed to identify them. For instance, the creature might (correctly) think its survival depended on its determining whether or not a particular sentence was a consequence of its beliefs, when in fact it could not perform this deductive task at all. (It should be noted that if the creature had truly unlimited deducing resources, it could squander them without ever running short and so need not satisfy the ideal heuristic requirement. In this light, it is easy to see why the idealizations entirely ignore heuristic competence.) We shall see that Hintikka is not alone in accepting conditions requiring ideal deductive ability of an agent; proponents of the thesis of the autonomy of the mental generally tend to employ such idealizations.

Acceptance of these idealizations drastically constrains predictive cognitive theory. It is important to see that, although the ideal inference condition is weaker than the deductive closure condition, it is still much too strong. The first problem resembles one mentioned earlier for the ideal general rationality condition; it is a feature of our actual everyday belief-attributing practice that we do not deny that a person has a particular belief set because he fails to infer from that set all apparently appropriate logical consequences—or even a feasibly small set of the apparently most useful consequences. Human beings often fail to identify inferences of this kind; it is common to say, 'If I'd only *asked* myself whether *q* was true, I could have figured that out and then done . . .'. And of course people often cannot perform such deductive tasks even when they have identified them. As an example (from second-order logic), many have wanted all their lives to know whether Goldbach's Conjecture is a consequence of accepted axioms of number theory, but this task has not yet been accomplished; nonetheless, we do not deny that these people accept the axioms.

Thus, we do not in fact use the ideal heuristic and deducing requirements when we attribute beliefs to people in actual circumstances. We distinguish "good enough" from "perfect." Furthermore, the fact that we do not use these ideal requirements is not just an accident of our particular culture, like our lacking a one-letter word for 'all'; the choice between minimal and ideal conditions is not arbitrary. Attributions of belief are not valueless for predicting behavior if only minimal, rather than ideal, rationality is required. But adopting the ideal conditions would prevent us from taking advantage of most of the opportunities for effectively predicting human actions on the basis of an attributed cognitive system, since we would then have no cognitive theory that was actually applicable to human beings. It is practically unfeasible, if not impossible "in principle," for us to predict human behavior to any significant extent on a purely neurophysiological or behavioristic basis—we would confront a quandary of Laplacean grandeur. Only a cognitive theory can have the required level of abstractness. Hence, acceptance of the ideal conditions is a refusal to attempt to predict in most situations, a sulk because of human finitude.

The single clearest indication of the extreme inapplicability of the ideal conditions is that if a creature did nonvacuously satisfy them, most tasks of the deductive sciences would be trivial for it. Furthermore, the idealizations deny the cumulativeness of scientific inquiry, that knowledge is acquired over time, with future discoveries depending on earlier ones. The idealizations reject the very fact that our shared inquiries have a history. Failure to satisfy the ideal conditions thus should not be belittled as just a result of sloppiness. The common comparison in economic theory of the principle of maximization of utility with the postulation of dimensionless, perfectly elastic spheres by the ideal gas laws seems correspondingly out of place. There is not even a significant probability above chance of the agent's choosing many of the actions that would maximize his expected utility (for example, when selecting the action involves a deductive task of the difficulty of the Goldbach's Conjecture case).

And there is no better reason to expect deductive omniscience of a large population of agents—for example, the scientific community—even if inquiry is pursued indefinitely, to some Peircean limit. Most surprisingly, as I shall discuss in chapter 4, an agent or community of agents that possessed the more imaginable forms of this ideal deductive ability would have to possess a decision procedure for (among other things) the predicate calculus, which, of course, Church's Theorem shows to be impossible. In many situations the relation of the ideal rationality conditions to actual human beings seems better compared, not with the relation of the ideal gas laws to real gases, but with the relation of phlogiston theory to actual gases. The departures of actual human behavior from the idealization are less noticeable to the human theorist, because he also cannot identify all the appropriate actions; those who supposedly use the pure idealization are thereby in effect often employing a theory of feasible inferences, as explained below.

The second way in which the ideal inference condition is too strong, then, is that it really excludes human beings from having beliefs; therefore, adopting the condition by itself excludes large ranges of prediction of human behavior. It is not much of a surprise that those who espouse idealizations that entail triviality of the deductive sciences end up committed to the impossibility of cognitive sciences.

A third way in which the ideal condition is too strong is that, for a nonsuicidal creature in the finitary predicament, it would be irrational even to try to satisfy it. Generally, there would be much more desirable ways for the creature to use its limited cognitive resources (such as those relating to immediate survival) than trying to ensure that every one of its actions is appropriate. I shall return to this point in section 1.8.

1.5 Minimal Consistency

The deductive ability required to satisfy the general minimal rationality condition must include not only an ability to perform useful inferences but also an ability to eliminate inconsistencies in the belief set. The belief set is subject to a *minimal consistency condition*:

If A has a particular belief-desire set, then if any inconsistencies arose in the belief set, A would sometimes eliminate some of them.

This condition applies both to explicit inconsistencies such as $\{p, -p\}$ and to tacit ones such as $\{p, p \rightarrow q, -q\}$.

Like all of the earlier minimal rationality conditions, the minimal consistency condition is specified by exhaustion of a trichotomy: an agent cannot permit all inconsistencies in his belief set, but he should be not required to eliminate every inconsistency that might arise in the belief set; hence, he must maintain minimal consistency. On the one hand, if an agent's cognitive system was not subject to some consistency constraint, and so could contain an unlimited number of inconsistencies, the attribution of such a system could not be of any value in predicting the agent's behavior. We could never expect such an agent, in accordance with the general minimal rationality condition, to attempt an action appropriate for a given belief; for this agent might in *any* case have another belief that was inconsistent with the given belief and that he might then act upon instead. A cognitive theory with constraints on only explicit contradictions, and not on tacit inconsistencies, would still be without empirical content for the same reason.

On the other hand, the minimal consistency condition must be clearly distinguished from an *ideal consistency condition*:

> If A has a particular belief-desire set, then if any inconsistency arose in the belief set, A would eliminate it.

This consistency condition is unacceptable for the same three kinds of reasons as the ideal inference condition was. First, it is clear that we do not in fact employ such a condition in our everyday psychology; the occurrence of a single inconsistency in a person's putative belief set does not rule out his having beliefs. Second, adopting the ideal consistency condition would not be advisable for the *attributer,* since it would amount to a refusal to attempt to predict behavior in terms of a cognitive system for creatures of anything like the human level of logical abilities: this ideal condition restricts the class of believers not employing extremely conservative strategies of belief acquisition to creatures for whom, again, a large range of tasks of the deductive sciences would be trivial. Third, the ideal condition requires an agent with human abilities and normal nonsuicidal desires to be irrational, in that there are often epistemically more desirable activities for him than maintaining perfect consistency.

This ideal condition seems to gain plausibility in a manner similar to the other ones: from recognition that some consistency constraint on beliefs is required, combined with not distinguishing minimal from ideal consistency. For instance, on the one hand, in "Psychology as Philosophy" Davidson states, "If we are intelligibly to attribute attitudes and beliefs, or usefully to describe motions as behaviour, then we are committed to finding in the pattern of behavior, belief, and desire a large degree of rationality and consistency" (1980b, 237). But on the other hand, the rest of Davidson's discussion strongly suggests that he thinks the possession of beliefs and desires requires perfect consistency, rather than just "a large degree" of it. For example, on the same page Davidson also says, "I do not think we can clearly say what should convince us that a man at a given time (or without a change of mind) preferred *a* to *b*, *b* to *c*, and *c* to *a*. The reason for our difficulty is that we cannot make good sense of an attribution of preference except against a background of coherent attitudes." Davidson is presupposing a particular "ideal consistency condition" on preference: that transitivity is never violated.

Quine's principle of charity in the interpretation of a speaker's utterances—for instance, "Fair translation preserves logical laws"—seems historically to have been one source of Davidson's acceptance of ideal consistency conditions. In fact, charity principles are rationality conditions. For instance, Quine's translation methodology itself presupposes an ideal consistency condition; in *Word and Object* (for example, pp. 57–61) Quine writes as if correct translation of the sentences a subject accepts must preserve ideal, rather than minimal, consistency (see section 4.10 below). And a similar consistency assumption seems implicit in Quine's holistic account of the structure of human knowledge in "Two Dogmas of Empiricism" (1961a, sec. 6; see also 1960, chap. 1). Davidson's transitivity condition, although still widely assumed in economic, game, and decision theory, seems to be simply false; people frequently speak and act in ways for which the best explanation is just that their preferences are inconsistent. In fact, much recent empirical work on the psychology of people's use of "quick but dirty" heuristics has focused on the widespread phenomenon of at least apparent breakdowns in consistency.[5] It should be emphasized that inconsistencies in a belief set need not be at all inexplicable. The logical relations among the beliefs involved in an inconsistency may be very unobvious and so not recognized; another important source of inconsistency is the structure of human memory, as explained in chapter 3. I will deal principally, however, with the minimal inference condition.

1.6 Vagueness

Having rejected the ideal inference condition, we can regard it as a provisional "ceiling" below which minimal deductive ability must lie. The specification of the minimal inference condition remains combinatorially vague; its structure makes every cognitive concept a cluster concept. The minimal inference condition by itself identifies, not a "simple defining property," but a cluster of properties for a creature having cognitive states—namely, apparently appropriate inferences the creature would make. With the possible exception of a "core" of obvious inferences (but see chapter 2), any one or more of these properties can be absent, and yet the creature may still qualify as having a cognitive system. But if all the properties are absent, the creature does not have a cognitive system; the "amount" of rationality cannot dwindle to a vanishing point. In the gray area between, the minimal conditions seem to be employed probabilistically.

One may wonder whether being minimally rational is not like being a little bit pregnant—an illegitimate notion, so to speak. What content can there be in rationality conditions that are so vague and context-sensitive? What fact of the matter can there be regarding whether a creature is rational enough to be an agent? But the boundary of a physical object is similarly ill-defined (under a microscope its surface is interpenetrated by the surrounding atmosphere, and so on). Yet we still bet our lives again and again each day on where such boundaries are —for instance, in crossing the street. The same point holds for where agenthood begins and ends. A gray area does not imply no distinction between black and white.

Dissatisfaction with the very form of the minimal rationality conditions may arise from acceptance of an oversimplified model of concepts. There is a tendency to treat all concepts as being like "bachelor" or "prime number"—that is, as defined by a single simple criterion. Also, vagueness is commonly regarded as absent from paradigm scientific theories, such as classical mechanics or axiomatizations of normative decision theory. A simplified notion of belief—for instance, that encountered in epistemic logic, where the deductive closure condition is used—is supposed to be preferable because of its formal manageability. In addition, the fact that a law is not precise and quantitative (as a physical law supposedly is) may be confused with its not having any predictive content. The indefiniteness of application of a vague term for intermediate cases restricts predictive value; however, it does not by any means eliminate it.

Real-world applicable concepts, as distinguished from some "pure" scientific idealizations, have a variety of uses, with correspondingly differing constraints. In this way, vagueness can sometimes have advantages. Since the belief-attributer, as well as the subject, is in the finitary predicament, he often cannot or ought not to obtain the evidence that would be needed to justify a perfectly precise assertion; accuracy here would be costly and unneeded. But there may be corresponding assertions employing the vague notion of minimal rationality that are justifiable by much less evidence, which it *would* be rational to obtain. Often an assertion regarding a certain topic—for instance, the fragility of an antique chair—will only be useful if made within an interval too brief to permit collecting the evidence needed to justify a precise assertion; yet such an exact assertion may not be needed—for instance, as a basis for warning someone not to sit on the chair.

1.7 Ancillary Theory

One may feel that, in any case, satisfaction of only a minimal inference condition would not provide as strong a basis as satisfaction of an ideal inference condition for attributing a cognitive system to a creature. For example, Davidson says, "We weaken the intelligibility of attributions of thoughts of any kind to the extent that we fail to uncover a consistent pattern of beliefs, and finally of actions . . ." (1984b, 11–12). The same view can be seen in Dennett's discussion of departures from ideal rationality: "As we uncover apparent irrationality under an Intentional intepretation of an entity, our grounds for ascribing any beliefs at all wane" (1978b, 285; see also p. 282). Above a threshold of minimal rationality, this does not seem correct; for example, failure to perform an apparently appropriate inference that is practically impossible—say, one that would take a human being more time than is available before heat-death of the universe—does not count at all against the person's having a cognitive system, if he makes enough of the easier inferences from those beliefs. In effect, 'ought' seems to imply 'can' in this case, in that the person cannot be required to perform inferences that are completely unfeasible. And we have a simple explanation of why the person cannot accomplish all inferences that are apparently appropriate for him—namely, that he has finite cognitive resources. Hence, the fact that a person's actions fall short of ideal rationality need not make them in any way less intelligible to us.

This leads to a more general point. Dennett may have had in mind something like minimal rationality conditions when he asked, "What rationale could we have . . . for fixing some set [of consequences of a belief that are themselves believed] between the extremes and calling it *the* set for a belief (for [any given subject] S, for earthlings, or for ten-year-old girls)?" (1978a,

21). In fact, for the minimal inference condition, this determination is based upon the attributer's understanding of the cognitive psychology of the particular subject, including theories of his deductive abilities and of his memory structure. In this way, minimal rationality conditions are context-sensitive. Let us briefly consider these two theories.

The content of the minimal inference condition—in particular, the minimal deducing requirement—is considerably increased when it is employed in conjunction with a weighting of deductive tasks with respect to feasibility for the reasoner. The cluster concept of minimal deductive competence has a typicality structure. That is, in everyday situations the attributer possesses an empirical theory, a profile of the difficulty of reasoning tasks for the human agent. This theory provides information on which inferences the agent ought to accomplish, namely, that easier ones are more likely to be performed. For instance, inferring $-q \rightarrow -p$ from $p \rightarrow q$ can normally be expected to be much easier than inferring $(\forall x)Fx \rightarrow (\forall x)Gx$ from $(\exists x) (\forall y) (Fx \rightarrow Gy)$. Thus, part of the answer to our main question—What is minimal rationality?—is provided by this *theory of feasible inferences*, which specifies more than just that some inferences must be accomplished. I will treat as an open question for the moment whether there are particular inferences—the most "obvious" ones, like *modus ponens*—that any creature that qualifies as a minimal agent must be able to perform. I will examine this "module" of our pretheoretical cognitive psychology in chapter 2.

When the minimal rationality conditions are applied to human agents, a theory of human memory structure further fixes the level of rationality required. In a human belief system, seldom can all things be considered. In predicting a person's behavior, it is very helpful to have some idea of which beliefs will be recalled when. In particular, a useful inference is weighted in terms of whether the beliefs that are its premises and rules are simultaneously "activated," or being considered, at a given time by the agent. If a human being is thinking at one "specious moment" about his beliefs 'If I drink the water, I will get sick' and 'I am drinking the water', it is at best a special aberrant case if he cannot then make the useful and easy inference to the conclusion that he will get sick. But a given inference, even one of the easiest like *modus ponens*, is evaluated as significantly more difficult if the agent has not yet "put together" the premise-beliefs. Failure to perform the inference in the former case is worse than failure in the latter case. In effect, there are two different minimal inference conditions; the activated belief subset is subject to a more stringent condition than the inactive belief set. As I will discuss in chapter 3, this weighting of inferences can be explained in terms of a fundamental model of *human* memory structure; it is easy to imagine agents that do not conform to this model.

The theory of feasible inferences and the theory of human memory structure are salient examples of the broad range of background cognitive psychological theory in which the minimal rationality conditions are embedded. These two theories extend the specification of what minimal rationality is for typical human agents and thereby help to set nonarbitrarily the "passing grade" for minimal rationality. The combinatorial vagueness of the minimal inference condition discussed in the last section is correspondingly reduced.

I will not attempt to enumerate the range of background theories typically taken for granted in using rationality conditions. But one additional important category of ancillary information consists of models of particular individuals. Human attributers seem to maintain ongoing projects of composing, in effect, huge novels-in-progress on each familiar person, detailing the individual's idiosyncratic personality traits, skills, pockets of incompetence, and so on. From the perspective of philosophy of everyday science, such an account of the quiddities of a human being does not seem so different from a record of the distinctive history and trajectory of a physical object like a billiard ball. In either case information on particularities greatly improves predictive power. Of course, for many kinds of reasons, including, as anatomists are fond of pointing out, that the human brain is the most complex structure presently known in the universe, there is no imminent danger of billiard-ball predictability of human action.

The holistic character of cognitive systems can be seen in the fact that they must attain a kind of minimum "critical mass." For example, it would be profoundly impossible for any agent to have just the single belief that $2 + 2 = 4$. This critical mass must also obey some structural constraints—as an example (besides the rationality conditions themselves, of course), we could not make sense of an agent that possessed either no desire set or no belief set. The contribution of the above ancillary theories to the content of the minimal rationality conditions illustrates the further holistic point that, by themselves, such rationality conditions can be used to make only limited predictions of actions on the basis of attribution of a cognitive system. Of course, the need for ancillary theory is not peculiar to everyday cognitive psychology. Physical theories similarly require a broad range of background assumptions—for instance, classical mechanics depends in this way on measurement theory.

1.8 Minimal Normative Conditions

We can make one final step in identifying what minimal rationality is. The set of inferences required by the minimal inference condition can be shown to be only a proper subset of the set of inferences that an agent ought to make if he is to be *minimally normatively rational*. Minimal normative rationality can be understood by considering two distinct theses concerning logical compulsion, each of the form 'In only some cases, if p implies q and A believes p, then A must (infer and) believe q'. (1) The descriptive thesis is the minimal inference condition: An agent must make some of the sound inferences from his beliefs that, according to his beliefs, would tend to satisfy his desires. The agent is required to make these inferences in order to be minimally rational—that is, in order to be an agent at all. In a case where p implies q, a person believes p, and the inference from p to q is apparently appropriate, the descriptive thesis predicts that at least sometimes the person must actually perform the inference; if he generally did not, he would not be a minimal agent and so would not qualify as believing p after all. (2) For our purposes, the normative thesis is this: The person must make all (and only) feasible sound inferences from his beliefs that, according to his beliefs, would tend to satisfy his desires. The agent is required to make each of these inferences *if* he is to be minimally normatively rational. In the case where p implies q, the person believes p, and the inference from p to q is feasible and apparently appropriate, the normative thesis says nothing about what the person will actually do; it says only that he must make this inference in order to be minimally normatively rational.

We can now explain the concept of minimal normative rationality in the following way. One sometimes encounters the claim 'If p implies q and a person believes p, then he *ought* to believe *q*'. For instance, in *Knowledge and Belief* Hintikka claims that it would be "indefensible" or "irrational" for someone to believe (or know) *p* and not to believe *q* here, in that he would be unreasonable and subject to criticism (1962, 29–31). However, from our discussion of the finitary predicament, it is clear that it is impossible for any real-world agent to make all of the sound inferences from the belief *p*; within limits, an agent can be rationally required only to make feasible inferences.

Furthermore, only a small subset of the sound inferences that it would be practically possible for the agent to make would be positively useful for him at a given time. An inference may be sound, but it may not be reasonable to make it, because it is of no foreseeable value at the time and prevents the agent from using his limited cognitive resources to do other things that are obviously valuable at the time.[6] Nobody lives forever. It would be a waste of a person's time—and in some cases insane—for the person to make many of the feasible sound inferences; a person could waste his entire lifetime, probably a short one, making only such uninteresting inferences. For instance, it would not be rational for a nonsuicidal creature to deduce vacuous consequences from one of its beliefs when this prevents it from making some other inference that would obviously yield information that at the time is crucial for its survival. As we have seen, there could be an infinite regress of inferences involved just in deciding which inference to undertake. *Not* making the vast majority of sound and feasible inferences is not irrational; it is rational.[7]

Therefore, it is true only in some cases that if *p* implies *q* and a person believes *p*, he ought to infer *q*, in that this is required for rationality. Hintikka's notion of rationality is narrow and excessively idealized, in that, although an agent could be criticized for a type of epistemic inconsistency, he might nonetheless be rational when practical limitations were considered. In determining whether the agent ought to make the inference from *p* to *q* in order to be minimally normatively rational, we must take into account not only (1) the soundness of the inference but also (2) its feasibility and (3) its apparent usefulness according to the agent's belief-desire set.

Even in those cases where the believer of *p* ought to infer *q* in order to be minimally normatively rational, there is no implication that a believer of *p* will in fact do this. The point for minimal normative rationality is the same as for Hintikka's much stronger notion of rationality (as he applies it to knowledge): "If [a person] knows that p and pursues the consequences of this item of knowledge far enough he will also come to know that q. Nothing is said about whether anybody will actually do so" (1962, 34). What is the relation of the minimal normative thesis to the descriptive thesis, the minimal rationality condition, which actually predicts what a believer of p will infer? The blurred set of inferences required in a particular case for minimal rationality is only a proper subset of the set of inferences then required for minimal normative rationality.

On the one hand, it should be noted that rejection of ideal rationality conditions therefore does not force adoption of an anything-goes psychologism of claiming "the organism is always right"; it is still possible for the minimal agent's actual behavior to fall short of what it ought to be, of minimal normative rationality. On the other hand, we do not deny that a person is rational enough to have a belief-desire set just because he forgetfully fails sometimes to make even the most obvious, and obviously apparently useful, inferences from the beliefs. As an example, I may have established earlier that $p \rightarrow q$; I may have been using it in other proofs, and so on. And I may now have just proved p; I may have been using it subsequently, and so on. And it may be that I must see that q is true before some other desired proof can be completed, but I may not have recognized this yet. Nonetheless, I can still qualify as believing p. Minimal normative rationality splits the difference between ideal and minimal descriptive rationality.

Thus, it is a fact of our actual belief-attributing practice that minimal rationality is weaker than even minimal normative rationality. Furthermore, one can argue that a satisfactory descriptive cognitive theory should employ rationality conditions that require less than "perfect" minimal normative rationality, as I have argued that the minimal rationality condition should be weaker than ideal rationality. Human beings and other intelligent creatures are at least capable of being moderately inefficient, forgetful, and careless (recall, too, the threatening regresses of heuristic decisions); consequently, without miraculous luck, they will make some bad decisions. Using the minimal normative condition as a descriptive condition would again exclude these creatures, although not so extremely as the ideal conditions, from having a cognitive system. This is undesirable because it would prevent the observer from taking advantage of most opportunities for predicting behavior on the basis of a cognitive theory, which is typically the only feasible means of prediction. In this way, the actual is not, and ought not to be, the ideal; minimal (descriptive) rationality should not be perfect minimal normative rationality. Not surprisingly, ideal rationality conditions, and hence the impossibility of predictive cognitive theory, gain plausibility when minimal descriptive rationality conditions are not distinguished from normative rationality conditions (this has seemed particularly noticeable in Davidson's and Dennett's accounts).

It is the concept of minimal normative rationality that is needed for a naturalized epistemology that takes account of the psychology and life situation—for example, the limitations, current beliefs, and goals—of the epistemic agent. I will explore consequences for Quine's naturalization program in subsequent chapters, particularly chapter 6. However, some of this basic perspective also seems apparent in work of Alvin Goldman, who proposes a reorientation of epistemology in the form of an enterprise of *epistemics* (see, for example, Goldman 1978). Epistemics "would seek to regulate or guide our intellectual activities" and would recognize that such "advice in matters intellectual . . . should take account of the agent's capacities" (pp. 509–510). Such a program rejects the concentration of traditional epistemology on ideal agents of virtually unlimited cognitive resources. When I have completed the outline of the theory of the minimal agent in part I, I will turn to its epistemological implications in part II.

After examining a range of rationality conditions, we have a first approximation of "How stupid can you be"—that is, of a minimal condition on the deductive ability required of an agent. Figure 1.1 shows the overall scheme for the various rationality concepts. I have focused on the "ceiling" on required rationality rather than the "floor," because the ceiling has been generally ignored. The ongoing project remains of further characterizing minimal rationality—for instance, by examining some of the ancillary theory employed in belief attribution, as I will do in the next two chapters. The sketch of a conception of minimal rationality we now have is by itself a step toward explaining the considerable success of human beings as behavior predictors, as in the Holmes story; we can see in this respect how everyday psychological practice can be so robust.

Furthermore, what we have found for commonsense psychology, however "primitive," should apply to more powerful

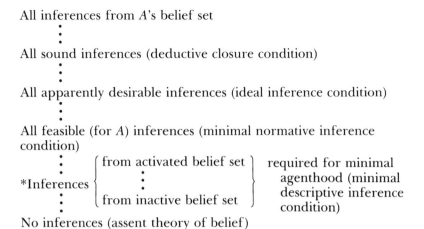

All inferences from *A*'s belief set

∴

All sound inferences (deductive closure condition)

∴

All apparently desirable inferences (ideal inference condition)

∴

All feasible (for *A*) inferences (minimal normative inference condition)

∴

*Inferences { from activated belief set ∴ from inactive belief set } required for minimal agenthood (minimal descriptive inference condition)

∴

No inferences (assent theory of belief)

Figure 1.1
Partial specification of minimal deductive ability

"scientific" psychology. It appears that any cognitive theory that is to satisfy the basic constraints of having significant empirical content, applying to finite creatures much more than "in principle" and being applicable by finite attributers, must include a *via media* fundamental principle that an agent has some, but not ideal, logical ability. Although minimal rationality conditions perhaps are not usefully regarded as "definitional," they must be distinguished from mere empirical generalizations about human psychology, such as a claim concerning human short-term memory capacity; we have seen that minimal rationality conditions have a centrality in a cognitive theory, such that they could not be rejected on the basis of just some supposedly contrary "data." The important point concerning the possibility and nature of cognitive psychology is that minimal rationality conditions seem indispensable in this way for satisfactory cognitive theory.

2

Feasible Inferences

What logical abilities must a predictive cognitive theory attribute to an agent? As we have seen, the assumption that the agent can make quite complex inferences from his beliefs is crucial in our pretheoretical attributions of psychological states in everyday situations. It has a similarly central, if tacit, role in conceptions of legal and moral responsibility, in historical explanation and economic theory, in philosophical accounts of meaning in terms of speakers' and hearers' intentions, and so on. However, I will argue here that very little of the deductive ability profile of a typical human being can be shown a priori to apply to all agents. The logical competence required of a minimally rational agent seems rather to have a cluster structure: it cannot be the case that a minimal agent is able to make no inferences, but the agent can be unable to make any particular one.

2.1 Role of a Feasibility Theory

By themselves, minimal rationality conditions can be used to make only very limited predictions of actions on the basis of an attributed belief-desire set. For instance, the minimal inference condition does not specify how long it would take an agent to perform a useful inference. If the attributer made the far-fetched assumption that inferences may take the agent up to some colossal amount of time, then the rationality conditions would cease to have content as a practical matter—for instance, as a basis for expectations that the agent will decide on appropriate actions. In addition, in predicting an agent's actions on the basis of his current beliefs and desires and the minimal inference condition, the attributer must answer the question, Which deductive inferences from the beliefs are most likely to occur? This question has two parts: first, what inferences are most likely to be undertaken (not necessarily consciously); and second, which of these are most likely to be accomplished (again, not necessarily consciously)? This chapter is concerned with the latter question, the feasibility of inferences once they have been undertaken, as opposed to the prior heuristic task of determining that particular deductive tasks will be appropriate.

Philosophy seems to have largely overlooked the point that without an extensive theory of the difficulty of different inferences, which provides information on which ones will be accomplished under given conditions, the predictive value of any attribution of a cognitive system of beliefs and desires would be severely limited. In our species some of this theory is probably an innate predisposition, and much of it is normally employed unconsciously as background assumptions. (In effect, some of it has lately become a debated issue in the design of computer natural-language processing systems that avoid obviousness mismatches in conversations with human users (see, for example, Joshi 1982).) Similar theories for second-order logic and nondeductive reasoning seem also to be important elements of our commonsense cognitive theory. For example, we can usually expect (unaided) people to infer quickly and reliably from 'There are 2 apples in that basket and 3 in this one' to 'There are 5 apples', but not so easily to infer from 'There are 298 apples in each of these 783 baskets' to 'There are 233,334 apples'.

In this chapter I will be concerned only with inferences of classical first-order logic (I will take up nondeductive abilities attributed in everyday explanation and prediction of behavior in chapter 5). I will refer to the theory of the difficulty of deductive inferences for an agent as a *theory of feasible inferences*. An easy inference is taken here to be one that would be reliably accomplished, given that it had been undertaken. Until the last sections of this chapter I will be representing an agent's beliefs as a set of sentences and an inference from those beliefs as the addition of a sentence to the set.[1]

Traditionally, for example in Descartes's *Rules for the Direction of the Mind* (1955a), "self-evident" or "clear and distinct" truths of reason, which are known directly and apparently reliably "by intuition," have been distinguished from truths that are not intuitively obvious. This distinction can be generalized in terms of the notion of an ordering of inferences with respect to relative difficulty. A theory of feasibility will include such an order-ing. Thus, other things being equal, inferring $p \rightarrow q$ from $-q \rightarrow -p$ typically is easier (and hence more likely) than infer-ring $(\exists x)\,(\forall y)\,(Fx \rightarrow Gy)$ from $(\forall x)Fx \rightarrow (\forall x)Gx$, and the latter task is much easier than one as difficult, say, as determing that the axiom of choice is independent of the other axioms of set theory.[2] An even more difficult inference would be one that required more space and time than is available before the heat-death of the universe. Of course, inferences involving sen-tences of the same logical form can differ in difficulty (for instance, two instances of *modus ponens* can so differ when the consequents of the two conditionals differ in complexity). The feasibility ordering can be roughly described as a well-ordering of equivalence classes of inferences. In particular, some infer-ences are (other things being equal) the least difficult, such as, typically, inferring p from $p \,\&\, q$; however, no inference is more difficult than all others.

2.2 Universality

Let us consider the feasibility ordering that in fact applies to some normal human being at a particular moment. The main question of this chapter concerns the universality of this theory. One formulation of this question is, What logical abilities de-scribed by this theory must be possessed by any creature that is an agent and, in particular, satisfies a minimal rationality condi-tion on deductive abilities? As discussed in chapter 1, minimal rationality conditions seem required for any cognitive theory that has predictive content and is significantly applicable to creatures of limited resources. This centrality of the rationality conditions must be distinguished from the status of true but low-level empirical psychological generalizations.

The question here is, What features of a theory of feasibility have a status like that of the rationality conditions—that is, a similar universality—and what features have only the status of a generalization about human psychology, or an even more limited applicability? The difficulty of an inference depends not only on the inference itself but also on the conditions under which it is performed. Feasibility orderings differ considerably among human beings (depending on training in formal logic, problem-solving "set," and so on); indeed, they can fluctuate for a single individual from one minute to the next, for instance, as he learns a new deductive strategy. It is false that the difficulty of any given inference is always the same for all reasoners, or even all normal humans. Consequently, the difficulty of an inference cannot correspond to any syntactical feature that is intrinsic to the inference, in isolation from the reasoning psychology of the deducer.[3]

There are several important empirical questions in the field of psychology of reasoning regarding the feasibility orderings of human beings. For instance, are certain logical operations or inferences easier for all "naive" humans with no training in formal logic? If so, which ones are natural or intuitive in this way? Authors of elementary logic texts often claim that they have chosen the inference rules and axioms of their deductive systems to be "convenient," "simple," and so on. A question for empirical research is, Which inference rules are in fact most easily learned and efficient for the purposes of formal deductions? One important impediment in empirical psychology of logic seems to be that there is uncertainty regarding the status of such questions—that is, regarding which parts of a theory of feasibility even need to be determined by empirical research, as opposed to some a priori transcendental argument.

The principal claim of this chapter is that there is greater latitude for such empirical investigation than has generally been granted. As we shall see, there seems to be a tendency in philosophy to treat contingent facts of commonsense psychology of reasoning as a priori universally applicable truths. However, it seems in fact that little of a typical human feasibility ordering can be shown a priori to apply to all agents; hence, we shall have to determine most features of the feasibility orderings that apply to human beings by empirical inquiry.

2.3 Alternative Feasibility Orderings

One source of uncertainty regarding whether assertions about the logical abilities of, say, a rational creature are a part of empirical psychology is the fact that features of a feasibility theory vary in their status. In particular, two alternative theories of feasibility are clearly ruled out as more than just a matter of empirical generalization. One of these alternatives is a *universal feasibility theory*, according to which every inference is maximally feasible, that is, always accomplished. This theory amounts to an ideal rationality condition; with such an extreme idealization of the logical abilities of an agent, no creature with fixed resources really qualifies as having beliefs. The other extreme alternative is a *null feasibility theory*, which consists of the assertion that every inference is maximally unfeasible, that is, never accomplished. The null theory simply says that all creatures that conform to it are entirely logically incompetent; therefore, by the argument of chapter 1 against the assent theory of belief, no such creature could have a cognitive system.

Thus, denials of the universal and null feasibility theories, and of approximations of them, are as universally applicable as the minimal rationality conditions on beliefs themselves. No empirical investigation is needed to justify rejecting the universal and null theories. The assertion of a pure universal theory that agents are ideal deducers generates so many incorrect predictions for any belief attribution that it thereby effectively excludes human beings (indeed, any finite creature) from having a cognitive system; the null theory directly excludes any creature from having a predictively attributable cognitive system. Feasibility orderings can and do often differ in "minor details," to some degree, from one human being to another. But we must now consider the possibility of certain alternative feasibility orderings that differ from, for example, some normal logically naive human's more than these common moderate variations, but less than the radically different universal and null orderings. Could there be an agent who conformed to one of these intermediate alternative feasibility orderings? These are the most philosophically important cases. According to these alternative theories, the inferences that are most easy for human beings, such as *modus ponens*, are evaluated as being of greater levels of difficulty—that is, as not being easy.

Let us consider the set consisting of all inferences from the least difficult for this particular normal human being through the least difficult ones that are practically unfeasible. One intermediate alternative to this person's feasibility ordering would be one in which this initial segment of the actual ordering was inverted: the easiest inferences became the most difficult within this initial segment, the most difficult inferences became the easiest in the new ordering, and so forth. According to the feasibility theory describing this alternative ordering, inferring q from $p \rightarrow q$ and p would not be possible, whereas performing an inference of the level of difficulty (for the original human agent) of determining the independence of the axiom of choice would be an easy task, performed reliably and without prolonged investigation. Supposedly, failure at the former task would be common, whereas failure at the latter task would be rare.

Thus, at the very least, typical human beings would be doing remarkably and inexplicably well at the more "difficult" inferences, such as inferring q from $p \rightarrow q$ and p, but they would always be failing at the "easier" inferences, such as the axiom of choice example. In this way, the alternative feasibility theory clearly would generate many incorrect predictions regarding the reasoning behavior of these people; anomalous failures and successes would be the rule. And so, in conjunction with the minimal inference condition, there would be strong empirical disconfirmation of any correct attribution of an explicit belief set to one of these people. (See section 2.7 for a qualification regarding nonverbal beliefs.) If a typical human's beliefs included 'If it rains, the dam will break' and 'It's raining', the alternative feasibility theory would imply that it was unlikely that the person would infer that the dam will break and act on this new belief (for instance, by seeking high ground); but in fact this inference and the corresponding actions would be very likely. And according to the alternative feasibility theory, we would expect particular actions that would be based on inferences that in fact would be very unlikely to occur; the actions would not occur because the required inferences from the relevant beliefs would not occur, and so again the correct belief attribution would be disconfirmed. Therefore, as long as, say, a Martian belief-attributer accepted an alternative feasibility theory of this kind, where a large initial segment of the feasibility ordering was inverted, a "normal" human being would not, according to the Martian's theory, qualify as having a cognitive system. This is not surprising, given the important role of a theory of feasibility in a complete cognitive theory, since by hypothesis this alternative was *false*—it did not apply to the subjects considered here.

The next question concerns the possibility of an agent whose logical abilities conform to this alternative feasibility ordering; in particular, could there be a creature that satisfied minimal rationality conditions but conformed to the alternative ordering? This would be a creature that, in relation to the feasibility theory for a typical human being, would in general not be able to perform any very easy inferences (for example, *modus ponens*) but would be able to perform many very difficult inferences like the axiom of choice example quickly and reliably, with a similar inversion of the intermediate cases.

2.4 *"Unnatural" Deductive Systems*

Certainly it is a fact of human psychology at least as basic as our having a short-term memory capacity of about six "chunks," or even a distinct short-term memory at all, that when we are naive about formal logic our deductive abilities do not conform to this inverted feasibility ordering. However, we must now consider some arguments for the stronger conclusion that a creature with anything like an inverted feasibility ordering is ruled out as more than just an empirical matter of human psychology. The first argument is that it would be much more difficult to explain how a creature could succeed in performing typically complex inferences (like inferring $(\forall x)Fx \rightarrow (\forall x)Gx$ from $(\exists x)(\forall y)(Fx \rightarrow Gy)$) but consistently fail at simple ones like *modus ponens*, than to explain how a creature could have a larger short-term memory than we do.

The mystery for the creature with the inverted feasibility ordering is, If this creature cannot perform any simple inference like *modus ponens*, then how is it able to perform much more complicated inferences? Such an argument might be assuming that, in explaining the creature's logical ability, we must use some Cartesian "principle of axiomatic method":

A deducer (or a deducer that is a rational agent) must generally perform complex deductive tasks by performing a sequence of simpler deductive tasks.

The more complex tasks would be taken here to be the more difficult inferences of a typical human being's feasibility ordering (like the above quantification-theoretic example), the simpler subtasks to be the easier ones in the ordering (like *modus ponens*). This principle therefore requires that an agent's problem-solving process for deductive tasks somewhat resemble the way in which a formal deductive system is used: simpler theorems are proven by employing elementary rules, and sometimes axioms, that are accepted as sound; other theorems are in turn proven by using these previously proven theorems, or by proving appropriate additional lemmas.

A creature with an inverted feasibility ordering seems to violate this requirement, since it is least likely to infer the "axioms" and simpler "theorems" and so will not use them in inferring the more complex "theorems," yet it can still infer these complex "theorems"—indeed, can infer them much more easily. A principle of axiomatic method does seem to be part of our commonsense psychology of problem solving in general, and of human deductive reasoning in particular—that is, the sort of deductive reasoning that even human beings who have never encountered a formal system perform. We do explain normal human performance of complex inferences as proceeding by means of simpler steps.

A reply to this type of argument is that it is easy to imagine a creature with "inhuman" psychological processes that would result in its having at least a very scrambled feasibility ordering with respect to the "normal" one but would still conform to this axiomatic methodology. Let us consider a hypothetical creature that exclusively uses a deductive system of axioms and inference rules in making inferences from its beliefs when it decides on actions. In particular, it does not "remember" and use previously proven theorems; it has this specific memory block (it has trouble thinking so abstractly), although it can still have other memory. The creature's system would consist of inference rules and axioms that would be unintuitive and complex for us; for example, an instance of one of the axioms might be '$((\exists x)Fx \to p) \leftrightarrow (\forall x)(Fx \to p)$'.[4]

It is clear that the inferences corresponding to each of these rules and axioms, which would be difficult for us, would be trivial for this creature. And if this deductive system was suitably designed, inferences that were easy for us would be possible but difficult using this system—they would involve many steps, special strategies, and so forth. Indeed, the latter feature is very common in the formal deductive systems found in elementary logic texts, despite efforts to the contrary: some of the inferences that are in fact the most trivial for human beings with no training in formal logic are much more difficult than some inferences that are normally much less intuitive. (For example, in Mates's (1972) system, inferring '$q \& p$' from '$p \& q$' is much harder than inferring '$q \to (p \to r)$' from '$p \to (q \to r)$'.) In this way, the logical ability of a creature that used this deductive system would approach an inverted feasibility ordering, and yet the creature would perform "easy" (for us) tasks by means of "difficult" (for us) tasks. The axiomatic argument against the possibility of a creature with an inverted feasibility ordering thus does not look promising.

For a second, even stronger reply to the above argument, we must first consider another creature that performs all of the inferences involved in selecting its desired actions by means of (a limit case of) a deductive system. This creature would employ only a list of theorems of logic (or substitution instances of such theorems), containing a finite number of items but including all theorems up to some colossal level of logical complexity. The items might be lexicographically ordered so that they could be searched efficiently. With this static list, the creature could perform any inference that an intelligent human agent could; this ability would suffice for all relevant actual or possible deductive tasks. Given any question of whether p is a logical consequence of a set (possible empty) of premises, the creature would form the associated conditional and search the theorem list. If the conditional was on the list, the creature would infer p from the premises; if it was not on the list (at the appropriate location in the ordering), the creature would not make the inference. Thus, this creature employs an "unnatural" deductive system consisting of an enormous axiom set and a single ("theorem") inference rule.

This system cannot be complete. But it would be practically adequate, in that the creature using it could have the logical ability needed to satisfy the minimal inference condition for having beliefs. Some creature of this kind could perform any deduction that a normal intelligent human being could; in fact, for any given creature with fixed finite resources, there would be some creature of this "unnatural" type with the same deductive abilities. However, it is clear that this creature's "all or nothing" feasibility ordering is not anything like the normal feasibility ordering for humans. The creature also does not conform to the above principle of axiomatic method. The creature would never follow the procedure of proving complex theorems by first proving simpler ones; indeed, the creature would never prove any theorems by first proving other theorems. (Note that assuming that some inferences must be made even in using the theorem list will also result in a type of regress similar to the Tortoise and Achilles (see Stroud 1979) for our own normal reasoning.)

Now, if all theorems of less than a given level of logical complexity (for example, of less than a particular large number of logical words in the corresponding schemata) are deleted from this creature's theorem dictionary, its logical ability will approximate (with allowance for its "all or nothing" character) the inversion of a normal human feasibility ordering. Thus, a creature that violated the principle of axiomatic method and conformed to a very different feasibility ordering, such as the creature of the last paragraph or this modification of it, is in fact possible.

The next question is whether such creatures could qualify as minimal agents—specifically, satisfy the rationality conditions. These creatures' procedure in performing a given deductive task might seem inefficient and heuristically obtuse, in that they could never use in accomplishing the given task any results they had previously obtained. Indeed, the creature's deductive procedure would be exceedingly computationally costly (see chapter 4); but our concern here, of course, is only with the intelligibility of such a creature. Perhaps these creatures could only survive in environments rather different from our typical terrestrial one; but that milieu has changed and will continue to do so.

It should be noted that the behavior of these creatures is not entirely bizarre; it differs only in degree from that of normal human beings. People sometimes, although not always, similarly use lists of theorems established by themselves or others, and use proof procedures. And humans often just forget, in performing an inference, to use results they have established earlier, even when the earlier results are obviously useful; consequently, there is inefficient repetition of effort. After all, the rationale for natural deduction systems is supposed to be that normal people in everyday situations find it difficult to reason abstractly and do not cite laws of logic. A "memory deficit" that only prevented learning new logic might be thought very peculiar. But brain-damaged patients who apparently can no longer transfer any new information from short-term to long-term memory (see, for example, Wickelgren 1968) still seem to manage to qualify as agents.

It seems that a creature of the above kind could accomplish enough of the inferences it undertook to qualify as having beliefs. Such a creature could in principle have sufficient cognitive abilities—in particular, be so fast in searching its theorem dictionary—that the inherent inefficiency of its deductive procedures would not, by itself, rule out its having a cognitive system. It also seems that a creature that searched its theorems effectively enough would satisfy any requirement on heuristic ability; it would undertake enough of the inferences that were apparently useful. Narrowly considered, a creature of this type would seem in one area to be heuristically imbecilic, in that the most obviously useful inferences (by any standard) would not be undertaken when their apparent usefulness was in accomplishing another deductive task. But if this creature's peculiar deductive process was rapid enough, there might in fact be no gain in efficiency to be had from its instead deducing as we normally do.

The minimal inference condition is only a necessary condition, on logical abilities, for having a cognitive system. To the extent that we regard satisfaction of the inference condition as possession of *all* of the logical ability required for having beliefs—that is, as a sufficient condition for being logically competent to have beliefs—satisfaction of the inference condition should permit the creature's satisfaction of other rationality conditions on having beliefs (including the minimal condition on belief-set consistency). (I will argue in chapter 5 that rationality by itself requires no nondeductive reasoning abilities, except for inquiry-selecting.) The above discussion then shows at least that a creature that is logically competent to have a cognitive system does not have to conform to the axiomatic method.

One response to finding that the above creature with its theorem dictionary could satisfy the rationality conditions may well be that this suggests the minimal rationality conditions are too weak; a complete or adequately rich cognitive theory would exclude so peculiar a creature. My strategy in dealing with this issue of completeness will be to consider several questions that arise concerning a creature with a radically different feasibility ordering. This procedure cannot decisively establish that such a creature could have a cognitive system; only a complete cognitive theory could do that. But this strategy will at least show that certain philosophically important theses underlying objections against the possibility of such an agent are mistaken.

Let us first provisionally draw the philosophical moral of the above discussion of creatures with inverted feasibility orderings. One point is that we must distinguish a psychology that seems radically different from our own, namely, that of such a creature, from a logically impossible or inexplicable psychol-

ogy. Perhaps we are innately predisposed to begin by project-
ing some "normal" reasoning psychology; but we can conceive
of alternatives. A creature whose deductive processes involved
the use of a suitable theorem dictionary would, without any
unaccountable mystery, manifest overt abilities conforming to
the inverted feasibility ordering. It seems at this point that, so
far as rationality is concerned, an agent must only be an adequate logician, not "the right kind" of logician; beyond empirical generalizations about human psychology, there is no particular right kind of logician. The cluster structure of the concept
of a minimal agent is apparent here for the logical abilities
required by the minimal rationality conditions. It cannot be the
case that an agent can make none of the inferences from his
beliefs, but the agent can be incapable of making any particular
inference.

2.5 Constitutive Inferences

The next type of question concerning agents with deductive
abilities radically differing from our own can be introduced by
the following argument: If a creature denies or suspends belief
in an obvious logical law like '$- (p \ \& \ -p)$', then it does not
understand the logical constants occurring in the law.[5] Understanding the constants (definitionally) requires accepting the
law, in the way that understanding the concept "bachelor" presupposes understanding the concept "unmarried." One question this argument raises is, What accounts for the alleged
special status of obvious laws like '$- (p \ \& \ -p)$'? Normal human
beings, of course, often accept some obvious laws and deny or
suspend judgment on many complicated ones, such as
'$(\exists y) \ (\forall x) \ (Fy \lor (Fx \to p))$'. We also have seen that there apparently can be deducers whose logical abilities are the mirror
image of ours—who accept many of the theorems we do not
and deny or suspend judgment on many of the theorems we
accept. Why would not their acceptance of those theorems constitute as good an understanding of the logical words involved
as our acceptance of other theorems? However, the argument
here can be reinforced by citing the difficulties in translating
and identifying the logical constants for deducers with supposedly radically different logical abilities. The conclusion of
the argument would still be that being able to perform certain
"easy" inferences is constitutive of understanding a given logi-

cal constant and therefore is necessary for believing *any* sentence containing that constant.

Let us consider an instance of this argument, namely, the claim that for the connective 'or', being able to infer $p \lor q$ from p ("'or'-introduction") and to infer q from $p \lor q$ and $-p$ ("disjunctive syllogism") are required in this way: in the simplest situation, if the deducer would assent to the premises but not generally to the conclusions of these inferences, there could be no basis for determining that the deducer meant by '$\lor$' or 'or' what we mean by 'or', as opposed to, for example, what we mean by 'and'. Whatever inference abilities remained could not be sufficient to distinguish 'or' from 'and' for this creature. For example, suppose (1) the hypothesis for some creature's inference behavior was that '*' was to be translated as 'or', although the creature did not generally infer $p * q$ from p, or infer q from $p * q$ and $-p$ as above for '$\lor$' (see table 2.1). And suppose (2) the evidence was that whenever the creature assented to $p * q$, it would assent to $q * p$ but not necessarily to r—that is, according to the hypothesis, the creature still had the logical ability to infer $q \lor p$ soundly from $p \lor q$, and not to infer r unsoundly from

Table 2.1
Interpreting '*': Some evidence

	Inferences involving '*'	
	the creature makes	the creature does not make
1	$\vdots$	$\dfrac{p}{p * q}$
		$\dfrac{-p \quad p * q}{q}$
		$\vdots$
2	$\dfrac{p * q}{q * p}$	$\dfrac{p * q}{r}$
	$\vdots$	$\vdots$
3	$\dfrac{-(-p * q)}{p * q}$	$\dfrac{p * q}{p}$
	$\vdots$	$\vdots$

p v q. This inference behavior would not provide any evidence that '*' was to be translated as 'or' rather than 'and', because the inference of q & p from p & q is also sound, and the inference of r from p & q unsound. The creature's inference behavior equally supports the hypothesis that '*' should be translated as 'and'.

The reply to this argument is that we must recognize that the inability to make "easy" sound inferences like p v q from p does not imply an inability to make other "harder" inferences; then it is clear that the argument does not show that for a deducer who does not make the two allegedly "constitutive" inferences for 'or', there can be no basis for determining that the deducer means by 'or' what we mean by 'or', as opposed to what we mean by 'and'. A creature that cannot make these two inferences may have enough *other* inference ability so that we can distinguish 'or' from 'and' for this creature. No question-begging is involved here; just given, for example, an object that behaved in the way we have described earlier as "having an inverted feasibility ordering," we could go on to establish the translation of logical constants for it.

Let us assume that we have established the translation of negation for this creature that seems to use '*' as a connective—say, that the creature means by '$-$' what we mean by it. Now, suppose (3) that whenever the creature assents to $-(-p * q)$, it would assent to $p * q$ (and whenever it assents to $-p * q$, it would assent to $(-p * s) * (-r * q)$, etc.). So long as we are assuming the creature has logical ability, this is evidence that '*' is to be translated as 'v' rather than '&', because the inference of p v q from $-(-p$ v $q)$ is sound, whereas the inference p & q from $-(-p$ & $q)$ is not (similarly for the other inference).

In the simplified translation situation we are considering, two types of inference ability provide a basis for determining that a deducer understands and uses a given logical constant. First, there are the sound inferences involving that constant that it will make, but that are not sound (and that it would not generally make) when another constant is substituted. Second, there are the unsound inferences involving that constant that it will not generally make, but that are sound (and that it would still make) when another constant is substituted. On the basis of these two types of evidence, we could similarly establish that the creature was using negation; and in this way we could also determine that the creature was using the universal quantifier.

Even if the creature used no other logical constants, it would then be able to express any sentence in which other constants occurred.

The failure of this argument against the possibility of a deducer that did not make the so-called constitutive inferences suggests that a cluster structure is again involved—here, in the identity of the logical constants. The meaning of the constants is at least partly determined holistically by the entire range of accepted laws and inferences in which they occur; this claim is just a special case of a post-Quinian holistic account of meaning (for example, a "conceptual-role" semantics). Quine (1970) says that the identity of a logical constant is determined by the accepted laws (more generally, let us say inferences) in which it occurs.[6] And Quine correctly points out that if for someone "all the laws which have up to now been taken to govern alternation were made to govern conjunction instead, and vice versa," the person's 'or' would merely become our conjunction, and vice versa (1970, 81). But Quine does not distinguish between rejecting *all* of the laws in which a given logical constant occurs and rejecting some of them.

We have found that, although a deducer cannot be incapable of making all of the inferences governing a given constant, it can be incapable of making any particular inference involving the constant (if it can make enough others) without changing the identity, and our translation, of the constant. However far-fetched the above creatures with deviant feasibility orderings may seem, and however unlikely it may be that these cases might arise in practical situations, they are important in showing what is necessary for the identity of logical constants. If we do not adopt the "cluster structure" view, we are faced with the problem of finding a satisfactory objective basis for the special status of "obvious" sound inferences or logical truths, as opposed to any other logical truths.

2.6 'Believing That ____'

One may feel that the account thus far of agents with radically different logical abilities from ours has been too syntactical or formalistic. I have been principally concerned with the expression '*A* believes '____"; that is, my account of the theory of feasibility has dealt with beliefs in sentences rather than, say, propositions. The criticism that this account is excessively verbalistic suggests that we should now also examine the expression 'A believes that ____'; for one might argue that creatures with radically different logical abilities from our own seem possible only as long as we deal solely with a creature manipulating sentences and so do not consider the latter expression.

This construction is of course referentially opaque—that is, intersubstitution of coreferring expressions after 'that' does not always preserve truth of the entire belief sentence. But is it "intensionally opaque"? Intersubstitution of synonymous expressions is sometimes alleged to preserve truth in this case; if a person believes that John is a bachelor, then the person believes that John is an unmarried male. Various "closely" logically equivalent sentences are commonly regarded as synonymous (or as paraphrases, or as expressing the same proposition), such as $p \& q$ and $q \& p$, or p and $- -p$. Therefore, by the intensional transparency claim of intersubstitutability of synonyms in belief contexts, for instance, if a person believes that $a = b$ and $c = d$, then he believes that $c = d$ and $a = b$.

Now, the objection against the possibility of a creature with, for example, an inverted feasibility ordering is this: if it is true that such a creature believes that $a = b$ and $c = d$, then by the intensional transparency thesis the creature must also believe that $c = d$ and $a = b$. It turns out, then, that in terms of the 'believes that ____' construction, the creature *cannot* have a deviant feasibility ordering, where this inference, which is obvious for us, is difficult for it (that is, not always performed). But according to the account of the theory of feasibility in this chapter, the creature (if it were a suitable English speaker) could believe the sentence '$a = b$ and $c = d$' while not (inferring and) believing '$c = d$ and $a = b$'. The objection here suggests that this disparity between the creature's believing that $c = d$ and $a = b$ but not believing the sentence '$c = d$ and $a = b$' must be resolved by abandoning the normal homophonic translation of the sentence. If a creature allegedly has very different logical abilities from ours, so that equivalences that are close for us are remote for it, then this requires us to alter our translations of its sentences so that its abilities conform to ours; otherwise, the above disparity arises. In this situation the 'believes '____'' construction must be used with caution.

The problem for the intensional transparency thesis that is relevant here arises when we ask, For whom must the intersubstitutable expressions supposedly be synonymous? Not for the agent; in the earlier 'bachelor' example the agent might not speak English and thus not know that 'bachelor' and 'unmarried male' are synonymous. Therefore, the intersubstitutable expressions must be synonymous for the attributer of the beliefs. If we do not consider a creature's psychology, all logical equivalences have the same status—those that are close for us, and those that are remote for us. The following counterexample to the intensional transparency thesis is based on the fact that that thesis permits intersubstitution of expressions that are synonyms for the attributer, but what are synonyms—and, in particular, closely equivalent expressions—for the attributer may not be synonyms, even in translation, for the agent.

Earlier we considered a case where a creature performed all of its inferences by means of a deductive system, and where this system, although sound and complete, contained only axioms that we (as normal human beings without training in logic) would find very counterintuitive (such as '$((\forall x)Fx \to (\forall x)Gx) \leftrightarrow (\exists x)(\forall y)(Fx \to Gy)$'). There are deductive systems of this kind in which it would be as difficult for an agent to determine the equivalence of p & q and q & p as it is for normal human beings to establish the equivalence of $(\forall x)Fx \to (\forall x)Gx$ and $(\exists x)(\forall y)(Fx \to Gy)$ (and vice versa); indeed, this holds to a significant degree for deductive systems in logic textbooks that are intended to be "intuitive" for normal human beings. Sentences that were closely equivalent for us and therefore synonymous would be remotely equivalent for this creature and therefore not synonymous for it, although it could still understand them—as we understand the pair of quantified sentences above.

Now let us apply the intensional transparency thesis to this creature with different logical abilities. Suppose that at some stage in a proof the creature believes that $a = b$ and $c = d$; and suppose that we are belief-attributers with "normal" logical abilities as characterized above, so that for us any sentence p & q is closely equivalent to and synonymous with q & p. Then, because the clause following 'believes that' supposedly is intensionally transparent, the creature believes that $c = d$ and $a = b$. But it is clear in this case that we, as attributers, cannot always project our particular logical abilities (as opposed to a general level of competence) onto an agent. Because of this creature's "abnormal" logical abilities explained above, it may *not* believe that $c = d$ and $a = b$; instead, it may be agnostic regarding whether $c = d$ and $a = b$.

What difference can there be between the creature's believing that $a = b$ and $c = d$ and its believing that $c = d$ and $a = b$? For, if the creature acts appropriately for the belief that $a = b$ and $c = d$, then it will *thereby* be acting appropriately for the putative belief that $c = d$ and $a = b$. The answer is based on the fact that genuine beliefs (in the "strong sense") must be casually efficacious: if an agent has a particular belief, then he not only must act appropriately for that belief but also must act in that way *because* of that belief; in particular, the belief must be part of the agent's reason for undertaking the action, one of the premises in the practical reasoning that results in the action. (Davidson (1980a,b) discusses this notion; see also sections 4.4 and 4.5.) We must distinguish between an agent's merely acting *as if* he had a particular belief and his actually having that belief. Although the logically deviant creature will act appropriately for the putative belief that $c = d$ and $a = b$, as well as for the belief that $a = b$ and $c = d$, only the latter will be its reason for these actions—that is, it will only use the belief that $a = b$ and $c = d$ as a basis for selecting desirable actions.

Given the creature's peculiar logical abilities, this situation is no more ruled out than the following case: a normal human being acts appropriately for the supposed belief that for the integers in a particular set, some x in the set is such that for every y in the set, if x is prime then y is odd; and he also acts appropriately for the equivalent belief that if every integer in the set is prime then every one of them is odd—but only the latter belief is the person's reason for those actions.[7] Whatever the complexities of the question of what constitutes a reason for an action, it is clear in this case that the person has only the second belief (there are similar cases involving logically valid sentences). The earlier '$a = b$ and $c = d$' case is similar; correspondingly, then, the creature in that case believes only that $a = b$ and $c = d$. If the similarity of these two cases is rejected, then the question must be answered, Why does the former case have its special status?

Thus the intensional transparency thesis seems incorrect: intersubstitution within the scope of a belief clause of expressions that are synonymous—in particular, closely equivalent—for the belief-attributer does not always preserve truth. Such intersubstitution preserves truth only on the following empirical assumption:

Expressions that are synonymous for the attributer correspond, in a correct translation, to expressions that are synonymous for the agent.

(The converse is not required.) This assumption is often an acceptable psychological generalization, but the above example shows how it can be violated. If we restrict this assumption to synonyms that are close equivalents, the assumption is a special case of the assumption that inferences that are obvious for a translator are obvious for the subject—that is, universality of the "lower" portion of the translator's feasibility ordering. The latter assumption is needed by Quine in his account of translation of logical laws ("Fair translation preserves logical laws," or better, fair translation preserves obvious logical laws), and it is unacceptably egocentric even as an approximation for practical purposes, for instance, when teaching logic to a novice. The original argument here against the possibility of a logically deviant creature must beg the question by assuming that there can be no such creature. Granting the limitations of the 'believes '___" construction, the 'believes that ___' construction must be carefully limited in application when the above assumption regarding synonymities does not hold.

The contingent status of the assumption regarding synonymities must be emphasized; the fact that p' and q' are not synonymous for a subject does not by itself rule out their translation respectively as p and q, where p and q are synonymous for the translator. 'Fair translation always preserves all synonymities' is not an acceptable maxim. This is a consequence of a moderate holistic account of meaning of the type mentioned earlier: the meaining of the expressions p' and q' is determined not just by the single ("analytic") equivalence $p' \leftrightarrow q'$ (or the corresponding inferences) but by the entire range of accepted sentences and inferences in which each expression occurs. In some cases we can establish that the correct translations of p' and q' are, respectively, p and q, if according to that translation p' and q' are involved in enough other laws and inferences that we accept in addition to $p \leftrightarrow q$.

As we saw earlier, there are some correct empirical generalizations regarding what equivalences are obvious or easy for normal "naive" human beings under certain conditions. But these generalizations have the same status as the assertion about short-term memory capacity. The most we can say is that certain inferences happen to be more intuitive or natural than others for normal human beings. We cannot conclude that any rational agent must think in these ways. Generalizations about which are the obvious equivalences are contingent cognitive psychology; a deviant creature, or merely a human being with training in formal logic, can violate these generalizations and still be a logically competent agent. Consequently, a theory of the meaning of an agent's assertions and a theory of what his beliefs are will not together be self-sufficient, contrary to Quine (1960); we cannot attribute beliefs and meanings without a third theory—of the agent's cognitive psychology, of how the agent represents and processes information.

2.7 Nonverbal Beliefs

One last question is, Could there be a feasibility ordering for a creature's inferences from its nonverbal beliefs that differed radically from our own? For example, could commutativity of conjunction fail for a dog's beliefs? In general, the feasibility ordering for a creature's nonverbal beliefs seems to a considerable extent to be a projection of the ordering for the attributer's verbal beliefs.[8] This is because in this situation there is no unique fact of the matter regarding what is the correct feasibility ordering and what is the correct formulation of the beliefs to assign to the agent; the two are to some extent interconvertible. The choice of a feasibility ordering here is then a matter of which one is not gratuitously complex; but this is a subjective matter, determined by what is familiar to the attributer. Therefore, for a verbal attributer with a radically different feasibility ordering from our own, the rational choice of an ordering to assign to a nonverbal creature (or to our own nonverbal beliefs) would generally not be our own.

Let us consider, for example, a Martian attributer with a feasibility ordering for its verbal beliefs such that for it the inference of $q \,\&\, p$ from $p \,\&\, q$ was as difficult or unintuitive as the inference of $-(p \,\&\, -p) \to (p \,\&\, q)$ from $p \,\&\, q$ is for us. Suppose that it is informed, and accepts, that Fido believes that it is dinnertime and a cat is on the porch. The assertion that our feasibility ordering universally applies for inferences from nonverbal beliefs will be false in this case; for this creature will not conclude that Fido believes that a cat is on the porch and it is dinnertime. And it would be as unnatural and gratuitous for it to do so, as it would be for us to conclude from the same original claim that Fido believes that if it is not the case that it is dinnertime and it is not dinnertime, then it is dinnertime and a cat is on the porch. Thus, it is a fundamental but contingent fact of *our* psychology that our own feasibility ordering seems to us to be the "correct" one to apply to inferences involving non-verbal beliefs.

Our general conclusion, then, is that the holistic interdependence of beliefs, desires, and meanings emphasized by Quine and Davidson in fact extends to another domain. Beliefs, desires, and meanings cannot be determined independently of at least a tacit theory of another type: a theory of the agent's cognitive psychology, of how the agent thinks. We have been concerned in particular with the theory of the deductive reasoning abilities of the agent, the theory of feasible inferences. A feasibility theory is an indispensable element of a predictive cognitive theory. For we have found that there seem to be remarkably few a priori contraints on a rational agent's deductive abilities. An agent must only be an adequate logician; beyond generalizations about human psychology, there seems to be no transcendentally "right" kind of logician.

3

Rationality and the Structure of Human Memory

What sorts of models of the agent's memory are presupposed in philosophical psychology and the theory of knowledge? What are more adequate—in particular, less idealized— models? In answering these questions, I will first argue that one cannot even explain important ranges of actual human behavior without employing models more "psychologically realistic" than conventional philosophical ones. I will then argue that an adequate understanding of the rationality of an agent's actions is not possible without such realistic models. The view that practical features of how we actually think are relevant to distinctively philosophical questions is by now familiar; examples are Quine's (1969a) program for the naturalization of epistemology and Goldman's (1978) more recent proposal of a philosophical discipline of "epistemics." And one natural response to this type of proposal is, I think, clear: Human beings are no doubt forgetful, careless, and so on; how can these failings be of interest to *philosophy*, as opposed to pedagogy, engineering, or other applied fields? The larger goal of this chapter is to illustrate how, when we examine the structure of human memory in some detail, and when we employ a theory of minimal, as opposed to ideal, rationality, we do obtain conclusions that are directly germane to basic philosophical issues.

3.1 Idealized Memory

Let us examine two examples of the type of idealization of the agent's memory that has been virtually universal in philosophy. The first example is Quine's influential model of the structure of the human belief system. That this idealization is present even within Quine's own program for naturalizing the theory of knowledge underscores the ubiquity of the idealization. In the last section of "Two Dogmas of Empiricism" Quine says, "Total science is like a field of force whose boundary conditions are experience. A conflict with experience at the periphery occasions readjustments in the interior of the field." In particular, "Reevaluation of some statements entails reevaluation of others, because of their logical interconnections . . ." (1961a, 42; see also pp. 43 and 44).

A natural "descriptive" interpretation here is that Quine is claiming that reevaluation of one belief entails reevaluation of others to maintain consistency of the total system, and that he is predicting that the proprietor of a belief system will in fact make the appropriate reevaluations. Given Quine's naturalism, one would expect that his account is intended to be descriptively correct. This interpretation is confirmed by Quine's later discussion of "the interanimation of sentences" of a belief system in the first chapter of *Word and Object*. Quine says of a portion of the belief system, "The theory as a whole—a chapter of chemistry, in this case, plus relevant adjuncts from logic and elsewhere—is a fabric of sentences variously associated to one another and to non-verbal stimuli by the mechanism of conditioned response" (1960, 11). Again, Quine seems to be describing the interconnections among an agent's beliefs in terms of predictions of changes in belief that really will happen, like the corresponding readjustments in the force field. Otherwise, the reference to "conditioned response" would not make sense.[1]

But the belief systems of actual human beings do not inevitably and automatically readjust themselves appropriately in the way Quine describes. The departures from Quine's idealization that we are concerned with here are certain types of forgetfulness; part of the human condition is in fact to fail to "make the connections" sometimes in a web of interconnected beliefs, to fall short of a synoptic view of one's belief system. For example, at least a decade before Fleming's discovery of penicillin, many microbiologists were aware that molds cause clear spots in bacteria cultures, and they knew that such a bare spot indicates no bacterial growth. Yet they did not consider the possibility that molds release an antibacterial agent (see, for example, Hilding 1975). As we shall see, what makes this common kind of example philosophically significant, and not just an unfortunate case of human sloppiness, is the way we can explain it. As a first "irrational reconstruction," we can say that the belief that molds cause bare spots seems to have been "filed" under the category of practical laboratory lore as information on undesirable contamination; the belief that a bare spot suggests inhibited bacterial growth seems to be in a different file, on microbiological theory. Thus, the web of belief is not merely tangled; its fabric of sentences is "quilted" into a patchwork of relatively independent subsystems. Connections are less likely to be made between these subsets. The Quinian model does not take into account the basic organization of human memory.

As a second example of the idealization in philosophy of the memory structure of the agent, let us briefly consider the "Preface Paradox" (see de Sousa 1976, 233, and Lehrer 1974, 203). If a person says F, 'At least some of my beliefs are false', it seems highly likely that he will be correct. The conflict that is sometimes felt arises because adding F to one's belief set guarantees that the belief set is inconsistent. Yet in real life people assert F-type propositions fairly often; for instance, in a book review of the *London Times Atlas of the World* Quine himself noted, without criticism, that "in a disarming gesture of realism" the atlas editors had included a back page for presently undiscovered errata (1981, 202). The seemingly overlooked point that is of interest here is that the *size* of the belief set for which a person makes the statement of error F determines the reasonability of his joint assertions. If he says, "Some sentence in $\{p\}$ is false, and p', this seems clearly irrational, like saying, 'I am inconsistent; I believe both p and not-p'. If he says, 'Some sentence in $\{p, q\}$ is false, and p, and q', this is similarly unacceptable. But if the set is very large, and in particular encompasses the person's total belief set, then accepting F along with that belief set becomes much more reasonable.

Why is the size of the belief set involved critical to whether the error assertion F is acceptable? If the person already thinks it is not merely possible but very probable—a moral certainty—that some of his beliefs are inconsistent, then he loses little by adding F to his belief set. Now, what model of human cognition accounts for why a large belief set is very likely to be inconsistent? Among others, the model that began to emerge in the discussion of Quine's idealized web would explain this: The total belief set of a human being is so vast that he cannot even exhaustively enumerate its contents. Furthermore, it is organized into independent subsets; inconsistencies between elements in these different "files" are less likely to be detected.

Thus, much of the perceived paradoxicality of the Preface Paradox seems to arise if one presupposes an idealization of the agent's psychology that is very like Quine's; and, to that extent, that apparent paradoxicality can be dissipated by adopting a more adequate model of human memory.

3.2 More Realistic Models

Let us examine such a model. One model that is significantly more satisfactory than the idealizations prevalent in philosophy has been employed in traditional psychology of verbal learning and memory for at least a century, continues to be fundamental in the more recent "constructive memory" and "semantic memory" approaches, and seems to be embedded even in our prescientific commonsense explanations of behavior. The model does not apply transcendentally to all possible rational agents; it is easy to imagine agents that do not conform to it—for example, Quine's idealized agent. An attempt to abstract from the sometimes conflicting versions of these empirical theories must be oversimplified and incomplete. However, the resulting rough picture is an important improvement over the philosophical theory; we are concerned with a matter of degree of idealization of theory.

The standard model in the verbal learning and memory tradition has a duplex structure; within a human being's memory at any given moment, a "short-term" or active memory and a "long-term" memory can be distinguished.[2] One major aspect of this distinction reflects the everyday observation that a person cannot, at one moment, think about all the information he possesses; he can only consider a subset of it. The contents of the short-term memory correspond to what he is now thinking about, not necessarily consciously (as when I drive a car properly while conversing about something else); all other remembered information is in the long-term memory. The storage capacity of short-term memory is commonly regarded as about six meaningful units or "chunks," such as randomly chosen words (Miller 1956). (The seven-digit length of telephone numbers was supposedly designed with this fact in mind.)

The duration of short-term storage of an item is also limited; the item is supposed to be remembered for less than half a minute if it is not "rehearsed" or repeated. The short-term memory is conceived of as a working memory, not just a passive store. That is, unlike long-term memory, it has contents upon which operations can be performed, such as making deductive inferences from the activated beliefs there; in particular, the practical reasoning from beliefs and desires that results in undertaking an action can only occur there. Constructive and semantic theories of memory include a similar conception of a short-term memory. It seems likely that there are several distinct special-purpose working memories and long-term stores. For example, nonconscious working memories are a basic element of psycholinguistic models of language comprehension and production. The "duplex" model can therefore be generalized as "n-plex," where $n > 1$.

In contrast to the span of short-term memory, the long-term memory is generally regarded as having virtually no practical capacity limit; also, some information can be stored there indefinitely. Therefore, long-term memory is where the vast majority of a person's cognitive system is at any given moment. Items can be recalled or retrieved from long-term memory to short-term memory—that is, copied into short-term memory without being erased from long-term memory. According to the traditional models, items in long-term memory are in "cold storage" and are virtually dormant; they can undergo none of the processing that items in short-term memory can (the model can be modified to include degrees of activation, as opposed to "all or nothing"). In particular, items there cannot affect behavior; for a belief to influence actions, it must first pass through the great bottleneck of short-term memory.

All of the accounts of human memory we are considering claim that the contents of long-term memory are organized. An item in long-term memory is located for retrieval not by a search of the entire memory but by a narrower search that takes advantage of the structure of the memory. All of these accounts in effect represent the long-term memory as a graph-theoretic entity, a network of nodes interconnected by arcs. The model is a generalization of the notion of a filing system, where a file can in turn contain subfiles. Each node is a storage location, containing a bundle of information. A search of long-term memory proceeds from node to node, via the interconnecting pathways; the search can be compared to running a maze. In the pure traditional theory the interconnections are associative links only; an example familiar from Hume is that, given one idea, which other ideas come to mind may be determined by bonds formed by past experience of the conjunction of that idea with other ideas. Consequently, much memory organization may be idiosyncratic to the particular person.

"Semantic memory" accounts, which have developed in computer modeling of human memory, include so similar a picture of the structure of long-term memory that they are sometimes characterized as "neo-associationist."[3] They generalize the interconnecting arcs to represent different kinds of relationships among the nodes; for instance, a directed arc between nodes n and m may represent that the item at n is an instance of, as opposed to a property of, the item at m. Also, memory structure can be dynamic: many different organizational systems can coexist, and the memory can be restructured for different purposes.

"Constructive memory" accounts emphasize that what is stored in long-term memory is not a fixed replica of an experienced event, such as the exact "surface" wording of an encountered sentence.[4] Instead, the underlying meaning of the sentence is integrated into the current memory representations or "schemata." These are therefore more than just a filing system for specific memories (the model resembles in some respects a "top-down" Kantian account of perception). Recall similarly is supposed to be a synthesizing process, in which one reconstructs, in the working memory, "what must have occurred" from a few fragments stored in long-term memory. For our purposes, the most important divergence of the constructive approach from traditional accounts is that for the former, information in long-term memory is not inactive; after acquisition and before recall a proposition may be assimilated to previous knowledge. The point remains that, for the constructive approach, processing in long-term memory is much more limited than processing in short-term memory (for some constructive accounts, this transformation of the stored item in fact occurs in a limited capacity working memory).

3.3 Commonsense Psychology

What model of human memory is presupposed by our commonsense intentional explanations of behavior? I have argued that we are able to understand and predict quite successfully an agent's actions on the basis of a prescientific cognitive theory that attributes a system of beliefs, desires, and other intentional states to him. I pointed out that the very possibility of a predictive cognitive science traditionally seems to have been denied because of covert acceptance of a conception of rationality so idealized that it is, for most purposes, not at all applicable to actual human beings. Our tacit everyday cognitive theory must include some other type of rationality condition; a concept of minimal rationality, where the agent can have a less than perfect ability to choose appropriate actions, is needed.

Basically, the prediction scheme involved here is this: The observer has attributed a particular set of beliefs and desires to a putative agent. Just to qualify as having that belief-desire set, the agent must attempt some of the actions that, according to those beliefs, would tend to satisfy those desires. That is, the agent must act minimally, but not necessarily ideally, rationally. The observer can identify this required set of actions and, if he has attributed the correct belief-desire set to the minimal agent, predict the agent's actions. However, this sketch of the predictive scheme still remains very incomplete. To predict an agent's actions in any interesting detail, the observer must know not just that the agent will undertake some of the apparently useful actions; the observer must be able to some extent to determine *which* ones. As noted earlier, the minimal rationality conditions in everyday practice are embedded in a broad range of other cognitive psychological theories that fill in where the minimal agent's behavior will depart from ideal rationality. One is the psychological theory of inference feasibility for the agent, sketched in the previous chapter. Another of the most important of these is a theory of human memory structure.

Although this commonsense theory of human memory may be more primitive than the latest theories of "scientific" psychology, it seems to share the two main elements that we have found in the latter theories. First, the tacit commonsense theory includes a short-term/long-term memory distinction. Only a small subset of the agent's total belief system, as the contents of short-term memory, can be activated or thought about at a given time; only these can influence the choice of actions and, in particular, be "logically processed"—used as premises for inferences or compared for inconsistency. The rest of the agent's beliefs, those in the long-term memory, are relatively inert. Second, the commonsense theory assumes an organization of long-term memory, one that determines the pattern of a search for an item and leads to some failures of retrieval to short-term memory. To predict significantly an agent's behavior on the basis of an attributed belief-desire set, we need to know which beliefs (and other elements of his cognitive system) are now in short-term memory, since they will otherwise be inactive; we seem to do so by using this memory model. (Indeed, some rudimentary representation of "psychological knowledge" of this kind has to be tacitly built into computer natural-language processing front ends for efficient interaction with human beings (for example, regarding how far back in a conversation a pronoun can refer).)

We employ this memory model to understand some very prevalent lapses from ideal rationality. I will not attempt an exhaustive typology of such lapses. One important kind of example: Jones may have proven that $a = b$ and also that $b = c$ at different stages of a long derivation. If asked whether $a = b$, Jones would then assent, and similarly for $b = c$. Jones has not forgotten either sentence; he still believes both of them. And yet it is a common enough situation for Jones then to wonder whether $a = c$ and not to be able to find out. When this occurs in ordinary life, we do not feel a temptation to say Jones did not believe that $a = b$ or did not believe that $b = c$. For we can make sense of this failure to make a very obvious useful inference from the two beliefs, in terms of the short-term/long-term memory distinction. When Jones reached the point in the proof where he asked himself whether $a = c$, he was not then thinking about $a = b$ and $b = c$. It was not the case that both of these beliefs were in short-term memory; hence, one or more of them was inactive, not capable of being used as a premise in reasoning.

Failure to acknowledge the short-term/long-term memory distinction seems responsible for most of the common denials in philosophy of the possibility of people making obvious logical errors. (As discussed in chapter 2, another main source is the a priori assumption that an inference that is obvious for the observer must be obvious for the subject.) An important example, as one might expect from the discussion of Quine's model of consistency maintenance, is Quine's principle of charity—in particular, his thesis that correct interpretation of a person's utterances must not attribute inconsistencies to him. Similar issues are involved in debates about whether a person can believe obvious contradictions. Another important case, especially prevalent in philosophical analyses of economic, decision, and game theory, is the requirement of perfect preference transitivity; an agent supposedly cannot ever prefer *a* over *b*, *b* over *c*, and *c* over *a*. A further example is the frequent claim that it makes no sense to say a person believes *p*, believes *p* → *q*, yet does not believe *q*.[5] All of these cases can be explained on the same pattern as the Jones example.

We also seem to explain some everyday behavior in terms of our theory of the specific organization of a given individual's long-term memory. For instance, Smith believes an open flame can ignite gasoline (he uses matches to light bonfires, etc.), and Smith believes the match he now holds has an open flame (he would not touch the tip, etc.), and Smith is not suicidal. Yet Smith decides to see whether a gasoline tank is empty by looking inside while holding the match nearby for illumination. Similar stories often appear in newspapers; this is approximately how one of Faulkner's characters, Eck Snopes, dies in *The Town*. The anecdote cited earlier about the nondiscovery of penicillin, and Duncker's classic experiments on problem solving, involve the same important type of lapse (see Wason and Johnson-Laird 1968, pt. I).

We can explain Smith's failure to infer the obvious conclusion that his match might ignite the gasoline, by use of a very plausible hypothesis about the taxonomy by which Smith's beliefs are organized at that time. We seem to assume that in Smith's not especially idiosyncratic categorization scheme, the belief that a flame can ignite gasoline is filed under, roughly, "means of ignition"; the belief that the match he now holds has a flame is filed instead under "means of illumination." The "illumination" category rather than the "ignition" category was checked because Smith decided he needed more light to see into the tank. The two crucial beliefs here (along with others) therefore were not both in short-term memory to be "put together"; but only if they were being thought about together could Smith make the connection and infer that there was danger. In this way, we have some idea of the relative feasibility of different recall tasks for a particular agent. Some of a human agent's departures from perfect rationality follow predictable patterns, understandable in terms of the organization of his long-term memory.

Less than ideally rational behavior like Jones's and Smith's is an uncontestable major feature of actual careful science (for example, many medical misdiagnoses), as well as of sloppy everyday life. However, instead of explaining, say, Smith's behavior in terms of the structure of his memory, one might try to argue that, at the time Smith lights the match, either he does not really believe that the match has a flame or else he does not then believe that a flame can ignite gasoline. For instance, in the former case Smith might just think the match was an illumination source and have no opinion about whether it was an ignition source.

One problem for this alternative account is that, if it is not to be just an ad hoc explanation for this one case only, it will entail a conception of a peculiarly indecisive agent. An agent often acts, as we would ordinarily say, inappropriately for one of his beliefs, whether because of forgetfulness, because of failure to infer a consequence of the belief, or for other reasons. Each time one of these inappropriate actions is followed by an action appropriate for the belief and vice versa, we would have to say that the agent had changed his mind regarding the proposition in question. Over an interval when we would normally claim the agent had one stable, enduring belief, we would instead have to say he very repetitiously kept temporarily changing his mind back and forth. It does not seem arbitrary here to prefer an explanation of the agent's behavior in terms of his memory structure to an account that makes his behavior just a patternless coincidence of wavering. (Of course, this does not imply that there cannot be genuine changes of opinion.)

I think the main motivation for the view that, at the fatal moment, Smith has no opinion about whether his match is an ignition source, and for a similar treatment of the Jones case, is acceptance of an ideal rationality requirement: Smith cannot believe that the match has a flame because if he did, he must—by the ideal rationality condition that he make all useful inferences—conclude that holding it near the tank is dangerous; and he does not do this. But we know that such an idealization requires the agent to have unlimited resources of memory and time; therefore, according to this idealization, Smith cannot really have *any* beliefs. The ideal rationality conditions do not seem a satisfactory basis for rejecting our earlier explanation in terms of memory organization. Thus, one way in which the psychology of memory is philosophically relevant is now evident. Without something like the memory model we have been exploring, philosophical accounts cannot explain, or even ad-mit the possibility of, a large and important range of human behavior, involving making obvious mistakes.

3.4 Two Standards of Rationality

Let us turn from the descriptive adequacy of this model to the normative issues of how a memory ought to be organized and of which actions an agent ought to undertake. One consequence of the model of human memory structure implicit in our commonsense cognitive theory is that there are two distinct levels of minimal rationality, one required for a person's inactive belief set and another, more stringent one required for his current activated belief set. The short-term/long-term memory distinction entails that only beliefs in short-term memory can be premises in reasoning; beliefs in long-term memory are inert— they do not interact with each other, and they do not affect behavior. Correspondingly, although beliefs in long-term memory are not free of all rationality constraints, more rationality is required of the beliefs in short-term memory. For example, we found no difficulty in understanding how Jones could believe $a = b$ and believe $b = c$ without inferring $a = c$, so long as the two beliefs were not both activated at the same time. But this would not be true if Jones were then considering both of these beliefs. If we asked him whether he realized that he had proven $a = b$ and that he had proven $b = c$, and he still claimed he did not see $a = c$, we would typically conclude either that he did make the inference—perhaps his claim was not sincere—or else that the two beliefs had not in fact been activated—perhaps he did not understand our question. That is, we do not always require even the most obvious useful inference to be made from inactivated beliefs; but for human beings (with the provisos of chapter 2), before we will accept that such an inference is not made from those beliefs when they are activated, we will reappraise the supposition that the beliefs are activated.

One might think the higher standard of rationality for short-term memory is just an idiosyncrasy of our commonsense cognitive theory that, fortunately, reflects the psychological facts of how our minds happen to operate. For instance, W. J. McGuire, in a paper on the empirical psychology of attitudes and beliefs, presented a model and several experiments on how people maintain consistency in their cognitive systems. McGuire sought empirical support for the claim that a person's belief set is subject to a "Socratic Effect," that is, that "a person's beliefs on logically related propositions can be modified by the Socratic method of merely asking him to verbalize his beliefs, thereby sensitizing him to any inconsistencies among his beliefs, and thus inducing changes toward greater internal consistency" (1960, 79). McGuire did not seem to be aware that much of his model is a special case of the conventional model of human memory structure; the "arena of consciousness" into which beliefs are recalled by the "Socratic method" and where they are compared for consistency corresponds to the short-term working memory. The Socratic Effect is an example of the higher level of rationality that applies to the contents of the short-term memory.

But a distinction should be made between a mere empirical generalization and a fundamental element of our cognitive theory. A more obvious case is that McGuire and many other investigators in the psychology of attitudes and beliefs include in their models an assumption that a person has a "need for consistency" and will attempt to maintain consistency in his belief set; they then treat this assumption as a low-level empirical hypothesis requiring experimental confirmation. But although there are important experimental questions in the field, the investigators seem unaware that if a putative agent does not attempt to maintain some consistency among his supposed beliefs, we will deny that he has any beliefs at all. This is one of the minimal rationality conditions on any belief system; we can be sure it applies before we try any experiment.

Similarly, it is not just a psychological accident that human short-term memory is subject to more stringent rationality conditions than long-term memory. Given that beliefs in human long-term memory are virtually inactive, the only opportunity for the beliefs of the total system to be logically processed and kept rational at all is in what happens to the belief subset in short-term memory. Whatever may be the minimum "passing grade" of rationality for the contents of long-term memory in a given case, if the activated subset did not exceed it, the long-term memory could not be maintained at that minimum level. This is because, as we have seen, the inactivity of the beliefs in long-term memory in itself degrades rationality. It results in the accumulation of unrecognized inconsistencies, valuable inferences not being made, and so on. Only the behavior of the contents of short-term memory can counterbalance the results of the inertness of the beliefs in long-term memory and so contribute to the maintenance of adequate rationality.

Thus, the Socratic Effect seems more than just a natural law of the human mind, such as the fact that our normal short-term memory capacity is six rather than twelve "chunks." Given the low quality of processing of the contents of human long-term memory, if someone were not more likely, for example, to discover inconsistencies among some subset of his beliefs, he would not be able to maintain enough rationality to qualify as having beliefs. This conclusion should apply for any creature, of human psychology or otherwise, that has a similarly duplex memory.

3.5 Efficient Recall

A correspondingly general conclusion applies to the other main element of the human memory model, the organization of long-term memory into independently activated subsets. I will argue that it is not just an accident of human psychology that the long-term memory is so organized; given the short-term/long-term memory distinction and some other basic constraints, the long-term memory could not be otherwise, or the total belief system could not maintain minimal rationality.

The first step in connecting long-term memory organization to minimal rationality is to note that minimal rationality of a duplex cognitive system requires efficient recall of items from the inert long-term memory to short-term memory. If only beliefs in short-term memory can control decisions, then a person cannot act minimally rationally—that is, to some extent appropriately according to his beliefs—unless, at least sometimes, the "right" beliefs are recalled to short-term memory. The right beliefs here are those that are relevant to making a current decision about whether or not to undertake a given action. For instance, it seems that just this type of failure to recall appropriate beliefs has occurred when Smith holds the match near the gasoline tank; given Smith's goal of self-preservation, his beliefs about whether a flame will ignite gasoline, and so on, are obviously relevant to the question of whether or not he should attempt this action.

Of course, Smith can still qualify in this case as having a belief system because his recall capacity, although not perfect in reliability and speed, might not be entirely inadequate. The most inadequate recall capacity would be a null one, where no putative beliefs were recalled from long-term to short-term memory; there would then in fact be no actual long-term memory. The next worst recall procedure would be one that operated on a completely random basis; that is, where "beliefs" were recalled but generally were unrelated to the current contents—for instance, goals and beliefs—in the short-term memory. Even if the contents of such a short-term memory (of normal human size, relative to long-term memory) satisfied some ideal rationality condition (for example, that any desired logical operations could always be performed), the relation of the putative total belief system to attempted actions would clearly disintegrate into chaos and fail to qualify as at all rational. Thus, there is some lower bound on recall ability.

How can the recall efficiency required for the minimal rationality of a cognitive system be achieved? This would be relatively simple if a person's belief system could be exhaustively searched in each case—for instance, in the situation Quine describes in the passages cited earlier, if, whenever I decided to add a sentence p to my belief system, I could check the consistency of p with every subset of my current total belief set. Given unlimited time, we could in principle perhaps make such complete searches to locate a desired item. But in fact, it is commonly taken for granted in the psychology of memory that we cannot retrieve in this way (see Howe 1970, 47, 55, and Lindsay and Norman 1977, 351); the simple fact that we often fail to recall desired information alone suggests this. The storage capacity of human long-term memory does not have well-defined upper bounds. The conventional view is that there are too many beliefs in the long-term memory for exhaustive searches. Further, the time available in which to identify desirable actions before the opportunity to benefit from them has passed is too limited. Even for a super-mnemonist with perfect retention, the problem of locating a needed item would remain, and indeed be worse.

Nonetheless, the unfeasibility of exhaustive memory search is not as basic a feature of our psychology as, for example, our finite memory capacity. We know that a cognitive system cannot be arbitrarily small—for instance, containing just a single belief. However, this holistic point still does not exclude the possibility of cognitive systems that are simple enough, and have rapid enough search procedures, so that exhaustive search would be practically possible. (Perhaps the belief systems of dogs and cats might qualify.) The point remains that the problems of maintaining rationality for such a creature would be fundamentally unlike those for a human being with a normally rich cognitive system. For instance, it would not be advisable for a normal human even to attempt an exhaustive search, if there were other valuable uses of his limited cognitive resources.

In the section of the *Treatise of Human Nature* on abstract ideas, Hume recognized the "given" for human beings of the unfeasibility of total memory searches. He says, "As the production of all the ideas to which [a] name may be applied, is in most cases impossible, we abridge that work by a more partial consideration, and find but few inconveniences to arise in our reasoning from that abridgement" (1965, 21). The question now is, On what basis can the search be abridged, given that we know that a random narrowing would lethally "inconvenience" our reasoning? Hume is also aware of this problem: "Nothing is more admirable, than the readiness, with which the imagination suggests its ideas, and presents them at the very instant, in which they become necessary or useful" (p. 24). However, Hume seems to overlook the same kind of point we have found overlooked earlier, that this "most extraordinary" ability is more than just a fact of our particular psychology; it seems a precondition for us to qualify as having a psychology, or beliefs (or ideas or concepts) at all. Nor does Hume attempt to explain what selection mechanism would be able to work so well; he simply concludes that it is "a kind of magical faculty in the soul."

3.6 Choosing an Inquiry

Hume's problem has wider philosophical significance. One may ask, How can I decide to recall to short-term memory a specific item currently in long-term memory, without *already* having the item available? (This question will recur in section 5.7.) The more general problem is deciding what to think about next. And this in turn is an instance of a rarely acknowledged but fundamental epistemological question, What should I inquire about? The answer must be relative to my current goals and beliefs about how to attain those goals. The most important point is that a creature that did no better than chance in identifying inquiries that were valuable for it would be a radically defective agent. Making a deductive inference was the kind of inquiry chapter 1 focused upon, as opposed to undertaking an empirical investigation, and the conclusion reached there in fact applies here: the random creature would in particular be a heuristic imbecile in its choice of deductions and therefore could not be minimally rational—that is, could not even be an agent.

The question of what we should inquire about cannot be ignored, because we are each in the finitary predicament, with cognitive resources that are severely limited relative to the range of possible inquiries. Of course, we cannot obtain and use all available information; furthermore, it would not be advisable to attempt to do so. A minimal epistemic agent could squander his lifetime collecting only uninteresting information. We must therefore try to determine the best use of our resources by deciding which information would be most useful to seek.

A predicament arises because the outcome of a decision about whether or not to obtain a parcel of information cannot be guaranteed in advance. Undertaking an inquiry is like undertaking any other action; it entails risks, costs, and benefits. The solution for this general problem, as well as for the special case of memory search, will involve doing better than chance, but not, of course, doing perfectly; "undershooting" and "overshooting" are unavoidable. This is because the basis for deciding what inquiry to pursue will typically be incomplete. Otherwise, no decision about further inquiry may remain—the agent may end up already having made the inquiry. In addition, there is a point of diminishing returns, beyond which there are better uses of the agent's resources than in refining his choice of inquiry. And since such evaluations are themselves a particular kind of epistemic project, the selection of such projects cannot itself always be on the basis of an actual inquiry, or there will be a regress of the sort discussed for deductive inquiry in particular in section 1.3.

An adequate evaluation strategy must deal with this dilemma of having to be neither too restrictive nor too lax. In a passage in the *Critique of Pure Reason* Kant seems to be aware of the general problem of determining the value of an inquiry but does not seem to perceive the dilemma involved:

. . . in the endeavor to extend our knowledge a meddlesome curiosity is far less injurious than the habit of always insisting, before entering on any enquiries, upon antecedent proof of the utility of the enquiries—an absurd demand, since prior to completion of the enquiries we are not in a position to form the least conception of this utility, even if it were placed before our eyes. (1929, A237, B296)

Kant regards any evaluation strategy as unfeasible, and he seems to imply that none is needed—that is, that the most liberal strategy possible would suffice, contrary to what we have found. In fact, some inquiry-selecting ability of this kind is a precondition for being an agent. Moreover, we *are* able to "form the least conception" of the value of prospective inquiries—for instance, in deciding sometimes whether a given area of investigation is relevant to a current project. Given that an agent cannot have a "tunnel intelligence," how can the "corner of his mind's eye" enable him to make choices that are better than completely random gropes? Let us return to the problem of efficient recall as an instance of this predicament.

3.7 Limited Search

What is required for adequate recall is a satisfactory partial, as opposed to exhaustive, search strategy. Since long-term memory is unmanageably large for total search, the strategy should involve full search of only a subset of the items in memory. It is a commonplace in the psychology of memory, as well as in the management of other large information systems such as libraries and computer memories, that suitable organization of the stored items makes locating items relevant to a particular question easier. This is the underlying rationale for the network structure that is generally proposed in models of human long-term memory, as well as for the cataloguing systems of libraries. In computer science the variety of search schemes is vast; in artificial intelligence the importance of "the problem of knowledge representation" and, in particular, the need to subdivide large knowledge representations have long been recognized.[6]

As in the case of the general problem of choosing an inquiry, the required strategy here must be better than chance, but need not, of course, be perfect; the latter would require prescience. Searches can be expected to fail frequently in either possible way: beliefs that turn out not to be currently relevant may be checked, and beliefs that turn out to be useful may be skipped.

How can this strategy have a better chance of success than random search—a search of an arbitrarily selected subset? For this purpose, the stored items must be organized into subsets according to subject matter, where items within a subset are more likely to be relevant to each other than items from different subsets.

Which of a given set of items should be stored and grouped together in this way—that is, which are related to each other—is not an objective matter; it need not be the same for every rational creature. To some extent, how the items should be organized depends on the questions the creature is likely to ask, because of its beliefs and goals. For instance, if p and q together imply r and it is likely to be useful, given the agent's desires and beliefs, for the agent to find out that r is a consequence of its beliefs p and q, then to that extent it is advisable for p and q to be in the same subset; however, this would not be so if the logical relationship among p, q, and r was not of interest to the agent. On the other hand, the inconsistency of a set of beliefs always makes them, to that extent, "objectively" relevant to each other, whatever the agent's other beliefs and desires, because of the rationality requirement that minimal consistency be maintained. For human beings, some of the basic features of this structuring should be the result of natural selection, since they would have been helpful for survival in any likely terrestrial environment (although they may cease to be, as the individual departs from hunter-gatherer conditions). The rest of the individual's particular organizational scheme is learned, some of it as part of the culture, but much of it as idiosyncratic and flexible cognitive habits based on past experience.

Unlike the strategy of exhaustive search, this strategy for local search cannot be guaranteed to succeed, but it would be faster. It is a trade-off of reliability for speed, one of a series of trade-offs of competing desiderata involved in satisfactory organization of memory. As we shall see, another "golden mean" concerns the size of the subsets. If they are too large, then exhaustive searches within a subset will take too long and will approximate the exhaustive strategy for the entire system; if they are too small, then the chance of selecting the wrong subset, and so missing a desired item, will be too great. (Hierarchically nesting the subsets somewhat ameliorates, but does not eliminate, this dilemma.)

In terms of the rationality conditions on a cognitive system, the major cost of structuring the contents of long-term memory in this way is that inconsistencies and useful inferences that involve beliefs in different subsets are likely to be unrecognized. For example, McGuire points out, "The appearance and persistence of cognitive inconsistency in the individual indicate a degree of 'logic-tight' compartmentalization in the human thinking apparatus, by virtue of which certain sets of cognitions can be maintained isolated from one another, without regard for their logical interrelatedness" (1960, 98). Logical relations between beliefs in different "compartments" are less likely to be recognized than relations among beliefs within one compartment, because in the former case the relevant beliefs are less likely to be contemporaneously activated, and, as we have seen, it is only when they are activated together that such relations can be determined. The result is that, as Herbert Simon had noted much earlier in another connection, actual human behavior "exhibits a mosaic character," a patterned lack of integration; "behavior reveals 'segments' of rationality . . . behavior shows rational organization within each segment, but the segments themselves have no very strong interconnections" (1947, 80–81).

As in his discussion of the Socratic Effect, here McGuire does not seem to appreciate the fundamental status of compartmentalization. He refers to the well-known studies suggesting that "authoritarian" types of personality favor compartmentalization as an ego-defensive strategy, and proposes that the "cognitive barriers" between compartments can be made "more permeable" by the Socratic method of asking subjects to state inconsistent opinions in close temporal contiguity. However, McGuire's compartmentalization of beliefs is just a specific instance of the general organization of items in memory into subsets. And we have seen that some degree of such structuring seems to be an indispensable feature of a satisfactory limited search strategy, rather than an easily eliminable human flaw. We can now appreciate both the costs and the benefits of this strategy; prima facie, the resulting behavior can be characterized as departures from rationality, but on the assumption that exhaustive memory search is not feasible, such memory organization is advisable overall, in the long run, despite its costs. Correspondingly, a person's action may seem irrational when considered in isolation, but it may be rational when it is more globally considered as part of the price of good memory management.

3.8 Diminished Returns

The search strategy of structuring the memory as subsets of related beliefs is a matter of degree. Two items are in different subsets or compartments if they *tend* not to be recalled together. There are then at least two ways in which one belief system might be more compartmentalized than another. First, one of the systems might have more compartments than the other. Second, both systems might have the same pattern of compartments, but in one system some of the compartments might be less "permeable"; the compartmentalization would be greater in that beliefs from different compartments would be less likely to be recalled and considered together. We now know that (1) if there is no compartmentalization, if there is an equal likelihood that any belief will be recalled in conjunction with any other belief, cognitive resources will be spread too thin. Some degree of compartmentalization is indispensable for adequate management of our large memories; otherwise, recall would be too poor for the supposed cognitive system of which the memory is a part to satisfy the rationality conditions.

But we have also seen that the cost even of useful compartmentalization is in unreliability of recall. And it is now clear that too much compartmentalization will be counterproductive for efficient recall. Extreme compartmentalization can exclude a belief system from satisfying the rationality conditions in two different ways. On the one hand, (2) if a would-be belief system is organized into too many "sharply defined" small compartments, it in effect disintegrates into unrelated fragments. Too many of the "beliefs" will be unlikely to be activated together, with the result that too many inconsistencies and useful inferences involving them cannot be recognized.

On the other hand, (3) if much of a putative belief system is organized into a few sharply defined large compartments, we may feel that, instead of chaos, there is a "split personality," with corresponding total belief sets that are each employed in different types of situations. These sets can overlap considerably and still represent distinct persons, if the inconsistencies and missed inferences within each of these sets are sufficiently fewer than those in the conjoint total set. It is commonly pointed out in the philosophy of mind that the set of mental entities that constitutes a person must fit together as a particular type of coherent whole. The point here is that a special case of this required integration is that a person's beliefs must satisfy the rationality conditions; in this way, too much compartmentalization of a cognitive system violates our concept of a person, even a "minimal person."

Thus, as compartmentalization increases, there is a kind of diminishing return. Not only is there a minimum limit on compartmentalization for adequate search efficiency; there is also a maximum limit. The cost of compartmentalization is some isolation of subsets of the belief system from each other, and the resulting lack of interaction can fragment the total system. The contents of long-term memory are subject to less stringent rationality requirements than the contents of short-term memory, but they are not permitted unlimited irrationality. Only a balance of compartmentalization of long-term memory enables a complete cognitive system to qualify as minimally rational. Given the small capacity of the short-term memory in which all higher-quality processing must occur, and the unfeasibility of exhaustive search of long-term memory, such "moderate" compartmentalization is required for any rationality.

It is also clear now that (4) a candidate for a belief set can fail to be adequately rational in another way, if it is just compartmentalized in "the wrong way," rather than too much or too little. Two sets can be compartmentalized equally in the above sense, and yet one may be adequately rational, whereas the other is not. The latter set would fail to be rational because it was not organized into subsets of related beliefs, that is, it was not so organized as to satisfy minimal inference and consistency conditions: too many apparently useful inferences and too many inconsistencies were not recognizable. This in turn would happen because the sets of supposed beliefs involved in those inferences and inconsistencies were not grouped together and thus were unlikely to be contemporaneously recalled. The fact that the "right" way to organize a cognitive system to some extent depends on the individual's desires and beliefs does not imply that anything goes, that any organizational scheme at all will be equally adequate for that individual.

We now have the solution to Hume's mystery of how partial memory search procedures can be adequate; no magic homunculus is necessary. We have found a connection between memory organization and rationality: a basic precondition for our minimal rationality is efficient recall, which itself requires incomplete search, which in turn requires compartmentalization.

Compartmentalization seems in this way a fundamental constraint on human knowledge representation. Even if there might be other satisfactory ways of solving Hume's problem, compartmentalization is not just a regrettable failing of human beings, a departure from rationality *simpliciter*. Narrowly viewed, it leads to irrational actions, but overall, given our limitations (in particular, the slowness of exhaustive search), memory ought to be compartmentalized. Global rationality requires some local irrationality. Just how memory ought to be compartmentalized depends on, as well as the agent's beliefs and desires, various parameters of the psychological mechanisms involved, such as search speeds. The above argument does not establish that the actual is the ideal, that typical human compartmentalization is in fact optimal; it only concludes that some compartmentalization is needed for minimal rationality. To that extent, we have justified the ways of God, Nature, or natural selection and man, to Man.

With the framework we now have, let us reconsider the highly idealized model of the agent's memory tacitly presupposed in most philosophy. Quine's conception of the belief system of the epistemic agent was on the dynamic model, from classical physics, of the equilibrium of a physical system; such a passive, homeostatic model seems very far removed from reality. A more adequate representation here would be at least an information-processing model. In terms of the latter type of model, Quine might be described as viewing the entire belief system as contemporaneously fully activated or processed in parallel; the contents of the short-term working memory would be the complete long-term memory. A slightly more realistic hypothesis would be that, although short-term memory capacity is limited, all and only the appropriate beliefs at a given moment are always recalled. Such an ideal retrieval efficiency would require at least that exhaustive search of the long-term memory be feasible. This would still be a fundamentally inadequate model, since the success of an actual search cannot be guaranteed; it is as uncertain as running a maze—that is, proceeding through the network structure of the long-term memory. We thus find several layers of idealization in this typical philosophical model.

Several kinds of problems arise when one employs memory models as idealized as Quine's. First, one cannot even make sense of an important and prevalent range of human behavior, making obvious mistakes. Second, one cannot understand the ultimate rationality of such lapses, as the cost in a trade-off for some indispensable benefits. Consequently, one will give unsound epistemic advice. For instance, Keith Lehrer's response in *Knowledge* to the Preface Paradox was that an agent should not accept the statement F, 'At least some of my beliefs are false', because that would ensure the inconsistency of his belief set (1974, 203). But when we reject the model of an ideally efficient memory, we can recognize that our belief set is highly likely already to be inconsistent—that is a moral certainty—and we can make sense of this fact and its overall rationality. Therefore, since the cost of adding F to our belief set is actually quite small, and F is very likely to be true (and it would not be a good use of our resources to try to guarantee that F was false, nor is it likely we could succeed), we ought to accept F.

In these ways, I have shown some of the philosophical significance of the psychology of memory, in particular, its indispensability for an understanding of rationality for a creature in the basic human predicament. In chapter 2 I reached a similar conclusion regarding the indispensability of a theory of the agent's reasoning psychology. Thus, more generally, to ignore the question of the "psychological reality" of one's model of how the agent represents and processes information is to exclude the possibility of a philosophically adequate account of rationality, or of notions such as belief, preference, and meaning that presuppose it.

II

Epistemological Implications

4

The "Universal Acceptance of Logic"

I now turn from the theory of the minimal agent outlined in part I to some implications of that account for the theory of knowledge. Let us begin with the epistemology of logic. When Quine says that "better translation imposes our logic" upon the beliefs of any agent we try to interpret, and, furthermore, that "the logical truths, or the simple ones, will go without saying; everyone will unhestitatingly assent to them if asked," it is natural to wonder about the universal acceptance of logic.[1] Let us consider the following version of the thesis: Any rational agent must accept a logic, that is, at least a sound and complete first-order deductive system. I will argue that the thesis is false under some natural and philosophically important interpretations. The discussion will identify some relationships between computational complexity theory, recent psychological studies of the formal incorrectness of everyday reasoning, and more realistic theories of rationality.

Prima facie, the pattern of complexity-theoretic results in recent years constitutes a kind of practical analogue of the classical absolute unsolvability theorems of the 1930s. The project that emerges is to find the philosophical implications of these results, just as we have been trying to interpret the classical unsolvability results. In particular, if complexity theory in some sense "cuts the computational universe at its joints"—providing a principled basis for a hierarchy of qualitative distinctions between practically feasible and unfeasible tasks—then we need to examine the idea that, in at least some interesting cases, rationality models ought not to entail procedures that are computationally intractable. Complexity theory raises the possibility that formally correct deductive procedures may sometimes be so slow as to yield computational paralysis; hence, the "quick but dirty" heuristics uncovered by the psychological research may not be irrational sloppiness but instead the ultimate speed-reliability trade-off to evade intractability. With a theory of nonidealized rationality, complexity theory thereby "justifies the ways of Man" to this extent.

To begin, what is, or would be, a universally accepted logic? At a minimum, the thesis would be that all rational agents accept *some* sound and complete set of axioms and inference rules for first-order logic, as opposed to a claim of the universal acceptance of a particular set of "fundamental" logical laws and rules or, even more strongly, a claim of universal acceptance of all logical truths. The weakest thesis, therefore, could be false either in that (1) an agent might not accept a complete deductive system (he might have a "cognitive blind spot"), or (2) the agent might accept only an unsound or even inconsistent system (for example, he might use some rule that did not guarantee preservation of truth in inference, perhaps a quick but dirty heuristic), or, more strongly, (3) every law or rule the agent used might be unsound or also inconsistent. I will deal almost entirely with classical logic. This is not to prejudge the issue of the adequacy of nonstandard logics; the case of classical logic is basic, and the argument should be generalizable to other logics. Whatever one's choice of logic, the prior, and usually unacknowledged, question is whether a sound and complete logic by any standard must in fact be the best choice.

4.1 The Ideal Agent

Let us examine the concept of a rational agent that is involved in the thesis of the universal acceptance of logic. We have seen that some rationality constraint on an agent's cognitive system is among the most fundamental laws of psychology. For instance, it is generally recognized in the philosophy of psychology that, although consistency may be the hobgoblin of small minds, consistency is a condition for having any mind at all. And the conventional strategy in the cognitive sciences has been first to adopt an extreme idealization of the rationality required of an agent and then, perhaps, if they are noticed, to explain away departures of real human behavior from the ideal model. As discussed in chapter 1, prevalent models of the agent require that the agent be a maximizer of expected utility, that is, that the agent satisfy an ideal general rationality condition. An agent who is able to choose his actions so well has to have a great deal of logical insight. In particular, he must satisfy the ideal inference condition: The agent would make all and only deductively sound inferences from his belief set that are apparently appropriate. Otherwise, for instance, he might miss some apparently appropriate actions.

Now, must an agent ideally rational in this sense accept a logic? For the agent to be able to perform all sound inferences that might turn out to be apparently appropriate and not to make unsound ones, he must meet Cartesian standards of perfection: he must in effect be both infallible and able to have an opinion on anything with respect to logic. Such an agent cannot accept an unsound or incomplete deductive system. If he accepts an unsound system for making some of his inferences, he will not be guaranteed to make only sound inferences, appropriate or otherwise; and if he accepts an incomplete system, he will not be able to make some sound inferences that might turn out to be appropriate. In either case he will not satisfy the ideal inference condition. Therefore, an ideal agent must accept a sound and complete logic if he is to perform required reasoning by means of a formal deductive system.

4.2 Undecidability

The ideal rationality conditions abstract from a fundamental fact of human existence: we are in the finitary predicament of having fixed limits on our cognitive resources, in particular, on memory capacity and computing time. The next most basic fact of our psychology, after our rationality, is that we are finite objects. The standard model in effect assumes, for such legitimate purposes as simplification of theory, that human beings have God's brain; for this ideal agent, much of the deductive sciences becomes trivial.

If we suppose that the agent is finite, there is still another liability for the idea of an ideal agent using only formal deductive procedures. Ideal rationality requires more than just use of a sound and complete logic. The agent must be able to use that logic very well, so to speak—so well that any given first-order sentence can be formally proved to be a consequence of a set of premises or proved not to be a consequence in a finite number of steps. Otherwise, the ideal agent would not be *guaranteed* always to succeed in making all needed sound inferences (for instance, any arbitrary inference he thought his survival depended upon) and also never to make unsound ones. (Nor could any recursive enumeration procedure by itself suffice, since the agent would wait forever for such a semi–decision procedure's answers without finding out that some inferences were unsound.) This finitely represented perfect formal ability, of course, would constitute a decision procedure for first-order logic, which Church's Theorem demonstrates to be impossible.

Hence, the ideal rationality conditions are very ideal indeed, in that they entail either the most basic practical impossibility— the use of infinite resources—or else a logical contradiction, like a square circle. Of course, the ideal rationality model remains an indispensable simplification of computational reality for many situations, for example, as one norm or "regulative ideal" for evaluating quick but dirty procedures. But care is required; using the idealization could be a bit as if Hilbert had retained the presupposition of formalism that all number-theoretic truths are formally provable "as a convenient approximation" in the face of Gödel's Incompleteness Theorem.

But perhaps the agent might accomplish deductive tasks by some entirely nonformal means, for instance, by immediate synthetic a priori intuition of the deductive relations among the propositions involved. The agent might do this by direct, quasi-perceptual, Gödelian insight into an independent realm of Platonic entities, or by means of his transcendental ego, situated outside of space, time, causality, and so on, as Kant and intuitionists such as Brouwer have identified it. Conforming to the ideal inference condition through such faculties of intuition may seem little better than doing so by means of an oracle or miraculously perfect luck in guessing; for example, physicalists and those committed to information-processing models of cognition may not be satisfied with even the form of "We are God's modem" explanations like these. These procedures remain in need of at least the outlines of a scheme of explanation: the alternative procedure must be one that guarantees inferential success nonalgorithmically. With intuitive access to a Platonic realm, it is no longer clear that an agent *is* restricted to finite cognitive resources, for instance, of time and space.

4.3 Computational Complexity

In fact, the deductive ability of the ideal agent is even further removed from computational reality. Even where there is no absolute undecidability, a kind of practical undecidability seems to extend further down, to the most basic parts of logic, to the very core of the notion of computation. In some respects, it is as if Church's Theorem applied even to the propositional calculus. Of course, a decision procedure exists for tautological soundness—for example, by use of truth tables. But although a tautology decision procedure is in principle possible, it now appears to be inherently "computationally intractable" and, in some sense, to be extremely unfeasible as a practical matter; for example, it seems to require computations for relatively simple cases that would exceed the capacities of an ideal computer having the resources of the entire known universe. What is the philosophical significance of such intractability?

The above tautology result is in the field of computational complexity, an area that has grown rapidly during the last decade or so and is yielding practical unsolvability results that may be as interesting in some ways as the classical absolute unsolvability results of the 1930s.[2] (Perhaps philosophy has overlooked the field so far because of a tendency to conclude that if a problem is decidable in principle, then it must be trivial, at least for philosophy conceived of as a "pure" nonempirical discipline.[3]) In complexity theory feasibility of an algorithm is evaluated in terms of whether its execution time grows as a polynomial function of the size of input instances of the problem. If it does (as does any familiar procedure for arithmetical addition, for example), the algorithm is generally treated as computationally feasible. If it does not and instead increases faster, usually as an exponential function (as does exhaustive search of the game tree in chess, for example), the algorithm is generally regarded as intractable.

Such intractability turns out to a large extent to be independent of how the problem is represented and of the computer model (for instance, random-access or deterministic Turing machine) involved. Just as Turing computability is a formal explication of our intuitive notion of computability, polynomial-time computability might be viewed as one formal specification of a pretheoretic notion of practical computability. As a first approximation, we can say that complexity theory thereby identifies some of the "natural kinds" of computational difficulty. I will turn later to the question of the "real-world relevance" of complexity theory; at least important exceptions must be acknowledged to any rule of thumb that equates real-world feasibility with polynomial-time computability.

The ideal agent's procedure for determining whether or not a sentence is a tautological consequence of a set of premises yields a test of whether or not a sentence is truth-functionally consistent. In complexity theory the latter question is known as the "satisfiability problem." Briefly, the relevant finding is that the satisfiability problem is a member of the very large and important class of "nondeterministic polynomial time" (NP) problems, which are known to be solvable in polynomial time on a nondeterministic Turing machine, which is allowed to make "guesses" and in effect has an unbounded capacity for some parallel computations. A problem solvable by a nondeterministic Turing machine in polynomial time is solvable by a deterministic machine in exponential time. NP includes P, the class of problems solvable on a standard deterministic Turing machine in just polynomial time.

Most important, the satisfiability problem is "NP-complete": *any* NP problem can be efficiently reduced to the satisfiability problem. Each one of the wide variety of known NP-complete problems, numbering in the hundreds, is similarly convertible into any other. In this way, the satisfiability problem is a "universal" NP problem. NP-complete problems have not been proven inherently to require deterministic exponential time; this is the major unanswered question, a "Goldbach's Conjecture," of the field, equivalent to the question whether NP $\neq$ P in that some NP problems are not in P. However, NP-complete problems are generally regarded as computationally intractable in this way, since only exponential-time deterministic algorithms for any of them are known, and since if they were not, so many important problems that have long resisted practical solution (such as the "traveling salesman problem") would then all turn out to be tractable.[4]

Thus, the ideal agent's perfect capacity even just to make all tautological inferences is the case par excellence of a problem-solving capacity that is strongly conjectured to require computationally intractable algorithms. Of course, a quick but dirty heuristic procedure for tautological inference will not necessarily yield such apparent exponential explosion of computation—presumably, that is how actual fallible human beings manage, as we shall see. But again, nonalgorithmic procedures would not suffice for the Cartesian perfection of the ideal agent, since ex hypothesi they cannot be guaranteed to work in all cases. A surprisingly small and basic fragment of the ideal agent's deducing ability seems by itself to require, for just a finite set of simple cases, resources greater than those available to an ideal computer constructed from the entire universe. There is another layer of impossibility between the idealization and reality, not merely minor exceptions.

4.4 Minimal Rationality

We can therefore say that, although use of an ideal rationality model is an understandable motivation for arriving at the thesis of universal acceptance of logic, some other argument still is needed for that thesis. Although ideal and more realistic models ought mutually to coexist, for some purposes the idealization strategy seems an overreaction to the "no rationality, no agent" point. The alternative approach is to begin with the somewhat less idealized, more realistic model of minimal rationality, where the agent's ability to choose actions falls between randomness and perfection. As we have seen, such a minimal agent must have some, but not ideal, logical ability— that is, he must satisfy the minimal inference condition: The agent would make some, but not necessarily all, sound inferences from his belief set that are apparently appropriate. (And the minimal agent must also *not* make enough of the inferences that are unsound or apparently inappropriate.)

A useful feature of this less idealized model of rationality is that it provides a philosophical framework for relating two areas of significant research during the last decade. One is the field of computational complexity. The other encompasses the many recent psychological experiments that suggest people's surprisingly ubiquitous use of prima facie suboptimal "heuristic strategies," rather than formally correct procedures, in everyday intuitive reasoning.[5] Although each of these areas has arisen independently of the others, there seems to be a fundamental connection: (1) Complexity theory provides a principled basis for raising the possibility that human beings (indeed, any computational entities) may not be able to perform some very simple reasoning tasks in ways that are guaranteed to be correct. (2) The empirical psychology of "irrationality" suggests how we can do these tasks, by showing something of how we in fact do them—by means of the quick but dirty heuristics. (3) The ideal rationality models are at best silent on the normative status of use of these heuristics; the minimal rationality model, to begin with, permits us to acknowledge the basic platitude that human beings are in the finitary predicament and therefore *ought* to use some such heuristics—according to this conception, formally incorrect heuristics need not in fact be irrational at all. They are not just unintelligible or inadvisable sloppiness, because they are a means of avoiding computational paralysis while still doing better than guessing.

The increasing interest in computational complexity and also in psychological heuristics makes it important to establish the status of claims of human (or even inherent computer) alogicality or illogicality. In particular, are the claims somehow a priori incoherent and so not a matter open for empirical study, as the rationality idealizations—and the usual charity principles—imply? We therby return to the issue of the universal acceptance of logic. Given the liabilities of the ideal agent concept, our main question has now become, If a supposed cognitive system qualifies as minimally rational, is there any sense in which it must include a logic?

To determine in what sense, if any, satisfaction of minimal rationality conditions implies acceptance of a deductive system, we must ask, What is accepting (or believing) a logical law or rule? Briefly, let us distinguish between strong and weak acceptance of logic. Assent to a logical law, mere lip service, is not enough to constitute strong belief in the law. Assent is neither sufficient nor necessary, although it is one type of evidence for such acceptance. In addition, acting appropriately for, or reasoning in accordance with, a logical law is not enough to constitute such belief. For instance, a sound argument is "in accordance with" *every* valid sentence, in the sense that the argument's conclusion also follows from the premises conjoined with any of these validities; there is then no distinction with regard to accepting logic between idiot and super-savant.

As Davidson (1980a,b) has emphasized, a belief must be part of an agent's reason for a decision. Causal efficacy, the "right" role in the decision-making process, also is required here; the minimal agent must actually use the law as a premise in some (not necessarily all) of the practical reasoning, conscious or unconscious, by which he would select apparently appropriate actions. (There can be important "generate and test" interplay between heuristic reasoning in the context of discovery and logic as post hoc tribunal in the context of proof.) The key notion in turn, therefore, is that of "using a logical law or rule" (the related notion of "following a rule" has of course received much attention since the later Wittgenstein).

In contrast, to accept or believe a logical law weakly is merely to be usefully (or instrumentalistically) described as using the law; it may be clear that the agent is not in fact using the law at all. This appears to be the sense in which Dennett says of adaptively behaving creatures from another planet that "in virtue of their rationality they can be supposed to share our belief in logical truths" and further, of mice and other animals, in virtue of their being intentional systems, that "whether or not the animal is said to *believe* the *truths* of logic, it must be supposed to *follow* the *rules* of logic" (1978a, 9, 11).

Thus, a person might strongly accept a logic—a small set of simple axioms and inference rules from which all logical truths could "in principle" be derived. But such strong acceptance of a complete deductive system for first-order logic is not the same as strong acceptance of "the theory of first-order logic": actual appropriate use of each of the infinitely many assertions derivable by means of those axioms and rules. However, although the latter is not possible for a realistic or minimal agent, the agent can resolve to accept, or be committed to accepting, these truths. Also, a person can endorse a deductive system—for instance, as an object language for the relatively restricted technical purposes of metamathematics. The more limited the use of the system—the more it is preached as norm on Sunday, but not practiced the rest of the week—the more such endorsement tends to fall below strong acceptance.

4.5 An "Epistemic Deduction Theorem"?

It may help to clarify the notion of strong acceptance if we consider the following argument that an agent must accept some valid laws or sound rules. One might reason from the agent's required ability to make some apparently useful sound inferences to his acceptance of the corresponding valid laws or sound rules, by appealing to a "quasi-deduction theorem." A version of the deduction theorem of the proof theory of first-order logic is that if ψ is provable from ϕ (where 'ϕ' and 'ψ' are variables ranging over sentences of a first order formal language), then $\phi \rightarrow \psi$ is provable from the empty set; that is, it is a theorem. An epistemic analogue is

If a sentence of the form ψ is provable by A at time t from a sentence of the form ϕ, then A accepts $\phi \rightarrow \psi$ at t.

One would then assert that, where ψ is a consequence of ϕ, if A is able to infer (or would infer) ψ from ϕ in even any of the "unsound" ways discussed earlier, then A accepts the logical law $\phi \rightarrow \psi$ or the corresponding inference rule; hence, in this case A strongly accepts the law or rule. The conclusion is then that an agent must accept logical laws and rules, namely, those corresponding to the inferences he is required to be able to make. The argument implies that an agent accepts more than just a nonredundant deductive system of a few independent rules and axioms; the agent accepts the large set of laws and rules corresponding to the many inferences he is able to make.

However, this "theorem" seems false. As an example, consider a person who frequently undertakes and succeeds in inferring $q \rightarrow -p$ from $p \rightarrow -q$. Suppose that this person in fact always performs this inference and all his other inferences by use of only elementary natural deduction rules such as *modus ponens* and *modus tollens*. And suppose that at the time the person *would* have similarly performed any other inferences, other things being as equal as possible. That is, it is not the case that he just happens not to think it is useful to perform any inferences in other ways but would have performed desired inferences in other ways if it had happened to seem useful—for instance, if not doing so would have resulted in obviously unfeasibly inconvenient proofs. I proposed in the last section that if a person strongly accepts a logical law, he would use it in selecting desirable actions; in particular, he would sometimes use it where it was apparently useful for such desired deductive tasks—for example, when it is practically indispensable for accomplishing them. In the above case the person does not accept '$(p \rightarrow -q) \rightarrow (q \rightarrow -p)$' or the corresponding inference rule; for he does not use either of these in performing desired inferences, even when such applications would be apparently useful, and he would not so use them. Instead, he uses and would use the elementary deduction rules.

This is clear if we consider a specific instance: the explicit steps written out by a person performing formal derivations, as opposed to the more problematic steps of his covert reasoning. It is common for a student learning a propositional calculus deductive system to reach a stage of competence at which he behaves as in the above example. That is, when he encounters deductive tasks where using the above contraposition theorem is permissible and appropriate, he instead uses the elementary rules—he cites only those rules as justification at each line of a derivation, and the lines conform to those rules. Using the contraposition theorem instead of the elementary rules in accomplishing part of a deduction might be very valuable (for instance, because of steps and time saved on an examination), and the student may have recognized that using some theorems instead of elementary rules would be very useful. Whatever the intricacies of the concept of using a logical law, it is clear the student is not using the contraposition theorem here.

And if the student would consistently behave in this way at this stage of his cognitive history—that is, his failures to use the theorem are not just occasional slips—then he does not then accept the theorem. It is also false that if he performs the inference, he *subsequently* accepts the corresponding law. It is common for logic students to have to persuade themselves over and over again of the soundness of an inference, because after each instance of making the inference they do not retain the knowledge that they have successfully performed it. Similarly, when a more experienced logician has performed a complicated deduction only once as a stage in some proof, he may not have a continuing belief in the associated conditional; for he may immediately forget his earlier result (and rationally do so, since it is unlikely to be useful later) and so have to perform the deduction again if the result again happens to be useful. Therefore, one cannot argue that an agent must accept some valid laws or sound rules by appeal to the claim that being able to infer, or actually inferring, a sentence of the form ψ from one of the form ϕ implies strong acceptance of $\phi \rightarrow \psi$ or the corresponding rule.

4.6 Practical Adequacy of a Logic

The question of universal acceptance of logic now becomes, Must a minimal agent accept a logic either strongly or weakly? The interesting issue is whether an agent's satisfaction of the minimal rationality conditions implies his strong acceptance of a sound and complete deductive system. (The argument below can also be adapted for the weak sense of 'accept'.) The question needs further sharpening: I have argued that, although a minimal agent must be able to make some sound inferences—that is, must have some deductive ability—he does not have to be able to make any *particular* inferences, even those that normal human beings find the most obvious.[6] But even if this is true, it does not exclude universal acceptance of logic. It might still turn out that any agent must strongly accept some complete set of valid laws and sound rules; it would just be that agents do not have to accept the laws and rules normal human beings do—for instance, those that normal humans find obvious. Our question is, therefore, Must a minimal agent strongly accept *any* set of valid laws or sound rules that constitute a complete deductive system, much less particular obvious laws or rules? It seems that an agent can have the deductive ability required by the rationality conditions without strongly accepting—that is, actually using sometimes—even one such law or rule. (I restrict consideration to verbally formulated beliefs.)

We need one more distinction. I will say that a deductive system is *metatheoretically* adequate if it is sound (and therefore consistent) and complete. In the first paragraph of "The Justification of Deduction" Michael Dummett asserts, "Failure of soundness yields a situation which must be remedied. Failure of completeness cannot always be remedied; a remedy is, however, mandatory whenever it is possible" (1978, 290). Dummett accurately describes adherence to such an absolute requirement as "the standard practice of logicians" in constructing and justifying formal logical theory. However, the metatheoretic adequacy of a deductive system must be explicitly distinguished from its *practical* adequacy: here, its adequacy for accomplishing the deductive tasks required of a minimal agent. If one assumes that any possible agent must be ideally rational, it is easy to overlook the difference between the two types of adequacy. But with a minimal rationality model, the divergence of the two types of adequacy becomes much more salient.

What is the relation between metatheoretic and practical adequacy? I will point out that practical adequacy does not require metatheoretic adequacy, that the former is sometimes preferable to the latter, and that the former may sometimes not even be compatible with the latter. The very quickest possible, but least reliable, way of performing a deductive task is just to guess the answer. We know that a minimal agent does not have to be a perfect logician, but the agent could not accomplish his required sound inferences (while avoiding enough unsound ones) just by a series of lucky guesses. There are, however, other ways to improve above chance the odds of selecting conclusions that follow from premises besides using a sound and complete deductive system. The agent might use what is in effect a better than random, but not perfect, gambling strategy for identifying sound inferences. Though such a rule of thumb would not always succeed, it might work sufficiently often to reach the break-even point of satisfying minimal rationality requirements. I will argue later that this type of strategy may be indispensable for avoiding computational intractability.

4.7 Against Metatheoretic Adequacy

The concept of such a strategy suggests, to begin with, that it is at least possible for a logically competent agent to have one or more "logical blind spots" that are the result of his exclusively using an incomplete deductive system (whenever he does use a deductive system). Given the difficulties for observer—and agent—in determining the agent's nonconscious cognitive processes, let us again consider the explicit steps written out by a person performing a formal derivation (or alternatively, the core dump of a computer running a theorem-proving program). As an uninteresting example, the agent might use a conventional textbook natural deduction system of independent rules, with a *modus tollens* rule that has a clause that excludes its application to formal sentences with more than 1,000 logical constants. Similarly, it is possible for an agent to perform all required sound inferences by means of an unsound, or even inconsistent, system. Frege's axiomatization of set theory in *The Basic Laws of Arithmetic* and Quine's in *Mathematical Logic* were both inconsistent in ways that did not reveal themselves to many who had used each axiomatization extensively. These two examples suggest that first-order deductive systems can correspondingly be inconsistent in ways that do not yield too many— indeed, any—unsound inferences for the range of deductive tasks required of an agent. And in fact, all the early formulations of the substitution rule for the predicate calculus are reported to have been unsound (see Kleene 1967, 107n, and

Church 1956, 289–290). (Of course, if a deductive system is inconsistent, it is complete, but this is no longer metatheoretic virtue.)

Furthermore, an agent who satisfied the minimal rationality conditions could use exclusively a deductive system in which *all* axioms were invalid and *all* inference rules were unsound. A natural deduction system corresponding to a standard textbook one but composed entirely of unsound rules can easily, if uninterestingly, be constructed. For example, to the original *modus tollens* rule a clause is added: 'When one of the premises contains more than 1,000 logical constants, the set of premise numbers of the line on which the conclusion occurs should be empty; otherwise, the premise numbers are as usually specified'. A similar premise number clause can be added to each of the other rules. Or the original other rules and the new *modus tollens* rule can just be conjoined as a single rule; such a matter of individuating rules seems arbitrary.

The agent would not use the usual shortcut "theorem" rule that permits entering in a derivation a previously proved theorem with an empty set of premise numbers. The claim here is just that this agent *can* exclusively use this set of unsound basic rules. The agent might happen to be uninterested in using that set to deduce "vacuous" valid sentences; perhaps, as empirical studies indicate for normal human beings (see the review in Cherniak 1984), he has difficulty reasoning so abstractly. As proponents of the naturalness of natural deduction systems often point out, outside of logic courses people rarely seem to use, or at least to cite, logical validities.

The unsound inferences permitted by this system would be performed relatively rarely because they would arise only under a restricted range of conditions: they involve very complex sentences, or might be otherwise unintuitive or difficult for the agent to perform. We know that an agent cannot perform all inferences—in particular, the more complex ones—anyway; so the unsoundness of this system need not detract at all from the agent's rationality. We conclude that metatheoretically adequate deductive systems are not the only way to achieve practical adequacy. One cannot argue that any possible rational agent must accept logic.

Furthermore, a stronger point against metatheoretic adequacy seems to hold: in important cases it is antagonistic to practical adequacy. A metatheoretically inadequate system could be superior to any metatheoretically adequate one for the practical purposes of accomplishing an agent's everyday deductive tasks, just as inconsistent naive set theory is often more convenient than one of the consistent axiomatizations. In such a situation, insisting upon use of a metatheoretically adequate system would itself be unreasonable, like demanding use of the more correct but hopelessly unwieldy quantum mechanics instead of classical mechanics for engineering calculations in designing a dam. Even outside of practical contexts, empirical theories are often recognized to be idealizations that are only approximations of reality and apply satisfactorily only over limited ranges of the parameters involved; the kinetic-molecular theory of gases is a standard example of an idealization that is employed because it is much more manageable than more correct theories that (for example) do not assume molecules are perfectly dimensionless spheres.[7]

Indeed, much evidence has recently emerged indicating that in a remarkably wide range of conditions human beings do not in fact use formally correct procedures in everyday nondeductive reasoning. And occasionally researchers in this field have pointed out, in effect, that use of such quick but dirty heuristics in practical as opposed to "pure science" situations may be a reasonable speed-reliability trade-off (see, for example, the last chapter of Nisbett and Ross 1980). There is also a separate tradition of empirical research suggesting that people do not use formally correct procedures in simple deductive reasoning. In addition, some of my own recent empirical studies indicate that subjects use a "prototypicality heuristic" in deductive reasoning, a set of shortcut strategies that exploit structuring of concepts in terms of prototypes, or best examples, of the concepts; we seem to extend the "context of discovery" in this way into the "context of proof." Furthermore, some of the evidence suggests that using this formally incorrect procedure is in fact rational, in that it pays off with lower error rates than formally correct procedures. These last findings are significant because they identify a connection between deductive reasoning heuristics and important work on prototype models of mental representation.[8]

Finally, it is worth recalling in this context the widespread occurrence of the simplest classical semantic and set-theoretic antinomies at the very core of our conceptual scheme, from the foundations of mathematics to ordinary discourse. This category of "data" may be another symptom of our use of formally incorrect deductive procedures. A revisionist history of logic should be worth exploring—one that, for example, examines more positive interpretations of Russell's Paradox than the traditional "Arithmetic totters" reaction of Frege.

4.8 Practical Paralysis

An even stronger point may hold than just that metatheoretically inadequate systems appear to be preferable sometimes to metatheoretically adequate ones. Some work on computational complexity raises the possibility that metatheoretic adequacy may in important ranges of cases be entirely incompatible with practical adequacy, both for some of the "pure" purposes of the deductive sciences and for the "applied" purposes of maintaining an agent's minimal rationality. Let us begin with an argument of Michael Rabin's for the introduction of a notion of probabilistic proof into mathematics.[9] Of course, no decision procedure is possible even in principle for all of elementary number theory, but even in-principle decidability can sometimes be of very limited value. Consider a result obtained by Albert Meyer and Larry Stockmeyer (Meyer 1975; Stockmeyer and Chandra 1979): Although the set of theorems of a formal system for the weak monadic second-order theory of successor (WS1S), a fragment of elementary number theory, is decidable in principle, its decidability seems extremely unfeasible in practice. The problem requires not just exponential time, but iterated-exponential time. To prove theorems of only 617 symbols or fewer would require a network with so many boolean elements that, even if each were the size of a proton (with infinitely thin interconnecting wires), the machine would exceed the volume of the entire known universe. In effect, the moral Rabin drew from the pattern of such complexity-theoretic results is that, to avoid the problem of unfeasibly long proofs, mathematicians sometimes should make the ultimate speed-reliability trade-off: relax the metatheoretic requirement of consistency, even where it is in principle satisfiable, to evade practical paralysis. Rabin recommended, and devised, methods of probabilistic proof that do not guarantee truth, but for which the probability of error can be determined to be, for instance, one in a billion.[10]

Rabin's strategy might be compared with undoing Descartes's

bargain; Descartes sought apodeictic certainty, but the cost is generally recognized to have been epistemic paralysis. We can extend the point from methodology of the deductive sciences to our concern about fundamental constraints on human cognition. There are now two possible extremes for dealing with (for instance) the problem of determining tautological consequence. Just guessing, the quickest but dirtiest procedure, is too dirty for even minimal rationality, since the odds of success are chance. The other extreme, a decision procedure, is the most reliable but also seems too slow; it is perfectly infallible, but it is probably computationally intractable, which may well be too slow for even minimal rationality. Therefore, a compromise between the two extremes seems needed to yield sufficient deductive capacity for minimal rationality.

Various trade-off strategies are in fact prevalent in computer science in dealing with problems that are found to be computationally intractable. Standards are lowered and "heuristic algorithms" and "approximation algorithms" are sought for the problems instead of perfect optimization algorithms (see, for instance, Garey and Johnson 1979, chap. 6). There is more than one type of compromise with perfect algorithmhood that might evade the apparent intractability of decision procedures for even just tautologous consequence. One might, for instance, use a metatheoretically adequate deductive system, but avoid worst cases by restricting its application to simpler special cases—sets of premises and a possible conclusion that are small enough so that the exponential explosion of operations is not severe. Therefore, the agent could never attempt to make an inference from, or to test for consistency, his entire belief set, or even a large portion of it. The cost, and the eventual limitation, is that the agent would then exhibit the most rationality "locally," within certain neighborhoods of his beliefs, and would be particularly weak on inferences and consistency involving beliefs distributed between such subsets. (In fact, as we have seen, a fundamental feature of human belief systems is that they are "compartmentalized" in this way; thus, an important additional rationale for this structuring is as a strategy for evading intractability.) Another, simpler strategy would be 'Given any instance of a deductive problem, employ the metatheoretically adequate system; if no answer results within some fixed time limit, just abandon the attempt and flip a coin to pick an answer'.

4.9 Real-World Relevance

These strategies, however, require that computationally manageable cases involving sufficiently large belief subsets be sufficiently frequent to avoid de facto computational paralysis. We must therefore turn to the issue of the "real-world relevance" of complexity theory. It should be emphasized that, at least at present, most complexity measures are not average-case estimates. Devising useful concepts of average-case algorithm behavior is in itself an interesting task, not to mention determining where they apply. The typical theorem stating that a problem is computationally complex is of a worst-case form: Given any algorithm for deciding each instance of the problem, each of an infinite number of cases requires exponential time.

This still leaves in limbo an infinite number of other cases of the problem. Which of them, if any, requires exponential time? Perhaps every instance of the problem takes exponential time; even then, the exponential blowup might be so slow that the computational cost is not severe for small cases of the problem. Or instead, perhaps no real-world relevant case—of less than colossal size—might require "serious" exponential time; the exponential cases might be of an input size that nothing of human-scale computational resources could ever even encounter. Or again, the problem's complexity profile might fall messily between these two extremes. Therefore, information is needed on the "density," or population distribution, of the hard cases. For example: (1) Do they arise "early" (for example, for cases of about the same order of size as the shortest decision algorithm for the problem)? (2) Do they arise "often," that is, within the population of interesting cases? This requires an understanding of which instances are interesting, which of course will be relative to particular goals. (3) How severe is the exponential explosion when it does occur? The probability distribution of relevant worst cases is presently not well understood.[11]

The Church-Turing thesis explicated the important but poorly defined concept of computability in terms of the formally well defined, and closely related, concept of Turing-computability. It would be natural to propose, analogously, a corresponding connection between our intuitive concept of *practical* computability and the formal concept of requiring only polynomial time. However, algorithms for linear programming are a well-known counterexample to the assertion that an algorithm is in fact practically feasible if and only if it requires only polynomial time. On the one hand, the simplex linear programming algorithm has been proved to require exponential time. Yet for decades the simplex algorithm has been found very usable in practice—for the population of problems of interest to its users. An "empirical" study of running times of the algorithm for actual problems in the banking, steel, and oil industries confirms this; and Steven Smale has proved that the exponential cases are in a sense rare. On the other hand, the "Khachian" algorithm requires only polynomial time, but its typical running time seems much worse than that of the simplex algorithm, because its polynomial bounds are so high.[12] The connection of polynomial time with in-practice feasibility thus needs to be interpreted with some caution.

Nonetheless, workers in many areas of computer science certainly continue to accept this connection as a very useful rule of thumb (see, for example, Garey and Johnson 1979, 8–9). And some rough estimates do not inspire optimism that methods like the above compartmentalizing and "give up and guess" strategies are by themselves sufficient to avoid intractability in the management of a human belief system. Even decidability of just the monadic predicate calculus (and of some other decidable subclasses of the full predicate calculus) is known to be "worse" than NP-complete: to require nondeterministic exponential time. (For a review of these results, see Lewis 1978.)

And at least as food for thought, it is worth again considering testing for tautological consistency, only a very small part of the general problem here, by means now of the truth-table method (even the more efficient known perfect test procedures such as Wang's algorithm or the resolution method still require as much time in the worst cases). How large a belief set could an ideal computer check for consistency in this way? Suppose that each line of the truth table for the conjunction of all these beliefs could be checked in the time a light ray takes to traverse the diameter of a proton, an appropriate "supercycle" time, and suppose that the computer was permitted to run for twenty billion years, the estimated time from the "big-bang" dawn of the universe to the present. A belief system containing only 138 logically independent propositions would overwhelm the time resources of this supermachine.[13] Given the difficulties in individuating beliefs, it is not easy to estimate the number of atomic propositions in a typical human belief system, but 138 seems much too low. Indeed, this might even be too "small-minded" for the minimum critical mass required for the belief set of anything we could call a full-fledged agent, especially when more realistically severe computational constraints are taken into account. Quinian and Davidsonian charity requirements that a translation be readjusted if it yields an inconsistent belief set already seem quite unrealistic in light of such "ten to the zillion"-step computational costs.

Furthermore, it is important to note that some exponential-time problems have been proved to have hard cases of small size (indeed, similar proofs have emerged for classical absolutely unsolvable problems).[14] As noted above, deciding WS1S sentences of just several hundred symbols is known to require more space (and time) than there is in the known universe. Also, Fischer and Rabin (1974) have shown that Presburger arithmetic requires nondeterministic exponential time and, furthermore, that the exponential explosion of proof length sets in early, for sentences of the same order of size as the decision algorithm.

Nonetheless, it is quite easy to show that an early onset of computational complexity—that is, for cases small enough to be humanly relevant—is not an inherent feature of intractability. Given any intractable problem with early-onset complexity, one can always construct another problem with complexity onset only for cases larger than an arbitrarily chosen size.[15] The significant implication here of this point is that "counting the horse's teeth"—empirically observing which are the interesting and difficult cases of a problem—will often be unavoidable; much of the "real-world" complexity structure of many intractable problems is at least presently a hybrid question, to be approached in the manner of McCall's study of the simplex algorithm cited earlier. In particular, researchers in artificial intelligence studying automatic theorem proving have valuable data on what are the "interesting," frequently occurring, cases of a given intractable problem, and which of them in fact require large expenditure of resources. Similar information can correspondingly be obtained for human deductive reasoning. That is, in the hypothetico-deductive manner, we can treat the issue of whether there is real-world relevant complexity at least as an empirical hypothesis, suppose it is true, and see how well its implications are supported by observations.

In fact, the rather wide range of recent evidence mentioned earlier seems to confirm that people actually do not use formally correct methods in their intuitive reasoning. Instead, they use procedures such as Kahneman and Tversky's "representativeness" and "availability" heuristics in nondeductive everyday reasoning, and somewhat similar "prototypicality heuristics" in deductive reasoning. Thus, the most fundamental "empirical" suggestion of complexity theory, that algorithmic methods of accomplishing even some very simple deductive tasks are likely to be intractable, would provide a unifying framework for explaining why we use such heuristics instead. It constitutes the ultimate "justification of the ways of Man" here. For a plausible conjecture to begin with is that our quick and dirty shortcut strategies are required to avoid intractability. To the constraint that information-processing models of cognition should be finitary, we could then add that, in at least some interesting cases, they also should not entail certain classes of computationally complex processes; this would be a further constraint on the deductive ability of the minimal agent schematized in figure 1.1. The possibility needs to be explored further that, to a considerable extent, the only way human reasoning (or any realistic agent's) can evade practical paralysis is by not using metatheoretically adequate deductive systems.[16] Ideal rationality requirements exclude even entertaining such a possibility as more than unimportant exceptions to a rule, but a theory of minimal rationality provides a principled basis for relating complexity theory and the psychological studies in this way.[17]

4.10 "Save Logical Truth"

Finally, let us return to the Quinian translation methodology with which this chapter began, and Quine's argument for at least the universal unrejectability of logic, rather than, more strongly, its universal acceptance. Quine's basic thesis is "Fair translation preserves logical laws" (1960, 59), truth-functional or otherwise; again, "I have insisted unconditionally that translation not conflict with any logical truths (*W & O* p. 58 ff.)" (1969e, 319). Quine seems to be claiming here that correct translation must not attribute to an agent rejection of *any* logical truth, that is, acceptance of the contradictory of any logical truth, which would of course be an inconsistency. Rather, we are obliged to construe, for instance, someone's putatively "heroically novel logic" so that he does not in fact "accept contradiction" (1960, 59). Such a translation principle is a version of the ideal consistency condition (of section 1.5) and excludes an agent from accepting even the most obscure inconsistencies (recall that Quine's own set theory in *Mathematical Logic* turned out to be inconsistent); this once more implies triviality of significant portions of the deductive sciences. But, although Quine may not seem perfectly consistent himself, he also asserts in *Philosophy of Logic*, "Save the obvious" (1970, 82). Perhaps the Quinian charity policy needs to be self-applied; Quine must really have had in mind the latter conception of "moderate," rather than perfect, charity. Thus: Save only obvious logical truths.

However, Quine seems to take back everything that is granted in this interpretation of "Save the obvious" by explicitly equating obvious and unobvious inconsistencies and logical laws. He says, "The logical truths are all either obvious [that is, "assented to as a matter of course"] or else potentially obvious, in the sense of being derivable from the obvious by individually obvious steps. . . . We see, then, how it is that 'Save logical truth' is both a convention and a wise one" (1969e, 318; see also, for example, 1970, 82–83). Quine seems, in effect, not to be distinguishing the infinite set of assertions of a deductively closed theory from the small set of obvious axioms of the theory. He is then able to conclude "Save logical truth"—that is, save *all* theorems of first-order logic—from "Save the obvious"—that is, save just the axioms. Nevertheless, let us keep distinguishing acceptance of only a complete deductive system for first-order logic from actual acceptance of each of the infinitely many truths derivable by means of that system, and therefore resume examination of "Save the obvious" without Quine's own gloss on it in terms of potential obviousness.

The translation principle is then simply 'Better translation favors the subject's not accepting the more obvious inconsistencies'. But the next question is, Are these inconsistencies to be obvious for the subject or, in translation, for the observer? The principle of charity that Quine says underlies the account of translating logic is that "one's interlocutor's silliness, beyond a certain point, is less likely than bad translation," where this "silliness" seems to be evaluated from the observer's perspective (1960, 59, 69). But the moral of chapter 2 was that we cannot egocentrically assume that what is startlingly false for the observer must be startlingly false for the subject. Quite unexotic situations constitute counterexamples to such an assumption of universality of obviousness—for example, what is obviously false for the logic instructor is unlikely to be so for the new student, or else there would be no need for the course.

Therefore, the translation policy must be 'Better translation does not attribute acceptance of inconsistencies that are obvious for the subject'. "Fair translation preserves logical laws" must now at least be correspondingly revised to 'Better translation does not attribute to the subject acceptance of the contradictories of logical truths that are obviously false for the subject'. A proper translation methodology must allow the possibility that the subject accepts the contradictories of logical truths that are not obviously false for him, just as Frege accepted his axiom of abstraction before 1903.

But if it is possible that the subject finds *no* contradictories of logical truths obviously false, then this translation policy no longer entails even a weak version of the thesis of the universal unrejectability of logic; rather, it is silent on rejectability of any particular logical law or rule. (Of course, no one could accept contradictories of all logical laws, any more than he could accept all logical laws, because of the sheer length of most of them.) Now, could a minimal agent find no contradictories of logical truths obviously false? The inconsistencies that, according to the minimal consistency condition of section 1.5, must be recognizable as obviously false by the agent need not be contradictories of logical laws (again, the agent may just not be proficient at reasoning so abstractly), since some inconsistent beliefs will only be particular instances of contradictories of logical laws. (For example, 'It's raining and it's not raining' bears this relation to the general schema 'p & $-p$'; see note 2, chapter 2.) Furthermore, we have seen that accepting and using contradictories of some logical laws sometimes may even be indispensable for the agent's minimal deductive ability. So far as the rationality conditions are concerned, a minimal agent might find no contradictories of logical laws obviously false and might reject any particular logical laws. The conclusion regarding even just the universal unrejectability of logic, as opposed to its universal acceptance, therefore seems negative: correct translation might attribute outright rejection of any particular logical truths.

The underlying weakness of Quine's translation methodology that is relevant here is that it restricts consideration to only translation of the subject's language and determination of the subject's beliefs. Thus, for example, Quine's indeterminacy thesis that the subject's beliefs and language are interconvertible, in that one cannot attribute beliefs without also assigning translations to the subject's sentences, under the constraint of a charity principle. But even where Quine grants translation is determinate—for logic—an observer cannot ascertain beliefs and translations without a third type of theory, of the subject's cognitive psychology. The observer cannot apply a satisfactorily moderate charity principle unless he has determined what is "startlingly false" for the subject. And, to determine this, the observer must take account of how the subject reasons, organizes his memory, and so on, along the lines of part I of this book.

Given the behaviorist zeitgeist at the time *Word and Object* was published, Quine's tendency to overlook this third factor is itself understandable, if no longer obviously correct to us. However, although such a motivation ought not to have force today, Quine's approach is not just his own idiosyncrasy; perhaps a Fregean heritage of antipsychologism has reinforced this tendency. As an important example, Davidson and others have espoused a more thorough holism than Quine's by insisting, within a decision-theoretic framework, that desires as well as beliefs and meanings must be considered together. But their holism stops here. The mental—that is, propositional attitudes and rationality constraints on them—is supposed to be independent not only of physical reality but apparently also of psychological reality—of how the agent actually represents and processes information.

However, such a wider theory of interpretation will still require a principle of moderate rather than perfect charity, and that in turn cannot be applied without taking into account the agent's cognitive psychology. It is in this way that a theory of interpretation is constrained to be "psychologically real." To examine the constraint that theories of propositional attitudes ought not in certain conditions to entail computationally intractable processes is just a more basic aspect of this turning away from an ultra-autonomist tendency. We have seen that this ultra-autonomism extends still deeper, excluding from consideration even the most fundamental fact of our psychological reality, that we have finite limits on our cognitive resources.[18]

The familiar debate about how to choose between competing logics (for example, which is more "natural") presupposes as an absolute requirement that we ought not even to consider "dirty logic"—in other words, logic that is metatheoretically inadequate. But we can now see that the commonplace that Dummett, for example, began with, that metatheoretic adequacy is mandatory whenever "in principle" possible, needs at least to be carefully restricted. If one is engaged in a metatheoretical investigation of a deductive system, rather than generally using the system, Dummett's assertion may be correct. An agent can endorse the use of a metatheoretically adequate system, reason about it, and even really use it in some limited contexts. But if the system is actually to be used extensively, metatheoretic inadequacy may be repairable only on pain of intractability; it would then be irrational even to try to adopt exclusively a metatheoretically adequate system, since that would preclude successful reasoning. It would be like insisting upon the perfectionism of the Cartesian method of universal doubt, with its resulting cognitive paralysis.

Thus, in contrast to Tarski's remark, "The appearance of an antinomy is for me a symptom of disease" (1969, 66), there is at least some truth to Wittgenstein's earlier image in his account of the (non)significance of the paradoxes, "A contradiction is not a germ which shows a general illness" (1976, 211). Contradictions need not *entirely* vitiate a system. Indeed, this chapter has gone further, proposing that inconsistency may sometimes be downright healthy. The moral regarding the thesis of the universal acceptance of logic is that, once we set aside extreme idealizations of the agent and begin to take into account at least the most basic facts of an agent's psychological reality, that thesis, like a number of other rationality idealizations, seems wrong, and interestingly so. Contrary to the usual charity principles, not only is acceptance of a metatheoretically adequate deductive system not transcendentally indispensable for an agent's rationality; in important cases it is inadvisable and perhaps even incompatible with that rationality.

5

The Special Reasons Requirement

Let us now turn to some implications of a theory of the minimal agent for an account of nondeductive reasoning. One of the central descriptive projects of the theory of knowledge concerns the question, What is required in everyday life for us to say that a person knows an empirical fact? At the start of the first *Meditation*, "Concerning Things That Can Be Doubted," Descartes asserted, "I ought no less carefully to withhold my assent from matters which are not entirely certain and indubitable than from those which appear to me to be manifestly false" (1955b, 137). Descartes then rejected all of his current beliefs, because they would be unjustified if he were dreaming or the victim of an all-powerful deceiver, yet he could not eliminate these possibilities. In contrast to the traditional Cartesian position, although without ever mentioning Descartes, J. L. Austin pointed out in "Other Minds" that we do not demand in real life that a person rule out *every* such possible challenge to his knowledge claim. As an Austinian ornithological example, typically when a person asserts, 'There is a goldfinch in the garden', his checking procedure in arriving at the claim can be subject to criticism as incomplete only to a certain extent: "Enough is enough: it doesn't mean everything. . . . It does *not* mean, for example, enough to show it isn't a *stuffed* goldfinch" (1979, 84).

The counterpossibilities to knowledge the agent is held responsible for are only those that satisfy a "requirement of special reasons": specific counterpossibilities that there is a definite basis for thinking might now apply. Thus, within our system of knowledge-gathering procedures, (1) the preliminary process of determining whether a counterpossibility to a knowledge claim is even legitimate to deal with must be distinguished from (2) the process of determining whether the counterpossibility in fact applies. Only counterpossibilities that pass the first "danger signal" check are supposed to be submitted to the second test.

The issue of excluding from consideration supposedly "silly" counterpossibilities does not arise only in the ordinary language critique of Descartes's method of universal doubt. We seem tacitly to be betting our lives every second on the vast unlikelihood of such possibilities. For instance, until a moment ago I unthinkingly took for granted that the floor would not open beneath me; from this perspective every breath drawn is a spin of the wheel. And indeed, the special reasons requirement is not just a museum piece of ordinary language philosophy: it seems to have an identifiable ancestry in common law (indeed, apparently as a kind of legal cross-cultural universal) and in American pragmatism, and to have generally unrecognized similarities to more current views of Neurath, Quine, Goldman, Dretske, and others. An idea so ubiquitously and independently conceived seems worthy of further examination.

An important epistemological question therefore is, How do we determine which are the legitimate or "real" challenges we must deal with? Rather than, say, focusing on the much-discussed issue of whether this requirement stops skepticism, or trying to find necessary and sufficient conditions for knowledge, I want to work out more of the "flowchart" by which we make these decisions. These everyday empirical knowledge-gathering practices possess a "some, but not all" moderate rationality structure that seems to mesh well with the type of nonidealized model of a minimal epistemic agent sketched in this book. The discussion here provides an opportunity to begin to extend that account, which has primarily concentrated on the deductive ability required of such an agent, to non-deductive reasoning.

5.1 The "Reasonable Person"

An important source of information on everyday knowledge-gathering procedures should be English common law, a set of doctrines (rather than formal statutes) that emerged from originally unwritten traditional legal usage. The idea that an agent is responsible for considering and eliminating only some relevant counterpossibilities to his assertions seems to correspond to the concept of negligence in Anglo-American jurisprudence. I focus here particularly on tort law (I will not review the legal theory of evidence); a tort is a civil, as opposed to criminal, wrong against a person.[1] The tort doctrine of the "reasonable man" is that a defendant is responsible for compensation of a plaintiff for such a wrongful act if the defendant is negligent: he is required to exercise "ordinary care," the care that a "reasonable and prudent man" would use to anticipate and avoid obvious possibilities for harm from his act. This doctrine relieves a defendant of liability for losses that occur in spite of such diligence—for example, because of extraordinary "acts of God" or a *lusus naturae* that would require superhuman abilities to foresee. Thus, the reasonable man doctrine has both a positive, obligatory side—a defendant is held responsible for exercising reasonable care—and a negative, exculpatory role—the defendant is not held responsible for more than reasonable prudence.

An assertion—say, of the safety of a vehicle—is one of the major types of act that can result in loss to another party. In this respect, the special reasons requirement thus seems a special case of the reasonable man doctrine. Of course, in any ordinary situation someone who carelessly asserts that a goldfinch is in the garden is not liable to be sued for damages; not enough is at stake to involve the legal apparatus of the entire community. Still, the basis for criticizing the claim as inadequately warranted seems to have the same structure as is involved in evaluating civil responsibility for a claim that an automobile's brakes are safe. In recent years American courts have been deemphasizing the concept of individual responsibility in tort law because, for example, liability insurance is viewed as diffusing costs throughout society, and because of the doctrine that the party with the "deep pocket"—the greater resources—ought to pay. Furthermore, common-law procedure is no algorithm; judges, and juries, often disagree. However, the key point here is that standards on an agent's performance that fall short of unequivocal perfection are not just an unwieldy philosophical contrivance; they have been used traditionally as a core element of procedures in a domain of great practical importance.

One of the most interesting features of the common-law standard of "reasonable care" is the procedures for reducing its vagueness or indeterminacy of application in actual practice. Major factors that determine the threshold of legally required care are the potential loss at stake and the judged probability of the loss's occurring under given conditions. For example, "very great care" rather than just "reasonable care" is required concerning seaworthiness and seamanship in operation of a boat for commercial passenger transportation, because of the risk of great loss of life (see, for example, Prosser 1971, secs. 5.31 and 5.34, and Baker 1979, 349).

Use of standards of negligence also involves a doctrine of diminished responsibility, in turn dependent on a theory of the competence and expertise of the agent. Along the lines of Aristotelian accounts of moral responsibility, children and those with mental disabilities, in virtue of being *non sui juris*—that is, not fully understanding the nature and consequences of their acts—may be relieved of legal responsibility for damage caused by their acts. For example, only such degree of care is required of a minor as is required of an ordinary child of the same age, judgment, experience, and intelligence under the same circumstances. Instead of being diminished, responsibility can be increased for adults with special professional expertise—notably, physicians, engineers, and lawyers in connection with malpractice. (In addition, as discussed in section 5.5, we seem to have a psychological theory of the relative feasibility of different inferences for a given category of agent.) What you know can hurt you, in particular, make you more responsible than the layman. Although these rules still inescapably involve fuzzy judgments of relevant similarity of circumstances, they constitute part of the basic strategy for setting norms for the level of care between all and nothing. They are another part of the commonsense psychological model of the "reasonable person" that we employ in everyday life.

5.2 "Transcendental" Rationale

The reasonable person concept is found cross-culturally and in many historical eras; correspondingly, the special reasons requirement seems more than just an idiosyncrasy of our particular common-law traditions. Furthermore, one can explain this evidence of universality by giving a sort of "transcendental" rationale for employing such procedures, that is, a functional explanation in terms of what is useful given the purposes of some important types of human social organization. (I shall also return to this rationale later in examining different formulations of the requirement.) For this discussion, I set aside skepticism and assume existence of the external world; I turn from the solipsist and individualist orientation of classical epistemology in terms of an isolated Cartesian ego to consider the social character of typical human knowledge-gathering and -transmitting processes.

In "Logic and Conversation" H. P. Grice (1975) identified a Cooperative Principle that seems to be the fundamental law of pragmatics, determining which linguistic utterances to others are appropriate (see also Austin 1979, 82). We assume that others, like ourselves, try to obey the rule 'Make only utterances that are most useful for the purposes of the current conversation'. Grice then proposed a set of subordinate conversational maxims that tend to fulfill the Cooperative Principle, notably here, 'Try to make assertions that are justified, and presently relevant'.

One can go on to argue that these pragmatic maxims are a virtually essential element of linguistic practice, reasoning along the lines of Kant's universalizability argument in the *Foundations of the Metaphysics of Morals* (1959) for keeping promises—that if people generally did not keep their promises, the usefulness of the entire institution of making and keeping promises would disappear. Correspondingly, in a society of confabulists and nonsequiturists, where people could not be assumed to be trying for justified and relevant assertions, one of the prime functions of language—conveying useful information—would be vitiated. Assertions based on just guessing, or unrelated to current purposes, would not serve this function. It is imaginable that the institution of language might still be worth having, but only for purposes such as entertaining one another by telling tales.

The claim that one of the main purposes of language is to convey presently useful information in turn presupposes that knowledge is not homogeneously distributed in the linguistic community. Although such a community certainly requires much shared belief, it is difficult even to conceive of a society in which there is a perfect equilibrium of belief, where no member has a belief the others do not share. Certainly a "face to face" pretechnological tribe would not qualify; perhaps a society of omniscient agents would. Individuals differ not only in exotic expertise but more commonly in being in better or worse positions to know particular things, by virtue of their current background and perceptual history and perspective. The hypothesis of a nonuniform distribution of belief or information in the community at any given moment motivates generalizing Putnam's (1975b) "division of linguistic labor" to a distribution of cognitive labor: in that wider way, two, or n, heads are better than one. A "society of solipsists," where members could seek only firsthand knowledge, would be profoundly crippled.

In order to use secondhand knowledge, each member must in effect possess a "cognitive Yellow Pages," a theory of expertise-distribution within the community—indeed, within a nested hierarchy of subcommunities. A competent member must know where to go—that is, when to trust the judgment or skills of others and how to call in someone who is more knowledgeable on a topic of present interest. Depending on the hearer's current calibration of a particular utterer as knowledge-gathering instrument in a given type of case, the hearer may be more or less confident than he would be if he had tried to establish a claim directly for himself. Of course, this highly structured information-propagation procedure works on the assumption that when an utterer makes an assertion, others can rely on it as more than a random guess. The usefulness of the whole system would wither if members did not generally attempt to meet, and could not expect others to meet, standards of trustworthiness in making assertions.

We can now return to the rationale for a requirement of special reasons for raising and dealing with counterpossibilities to knowledge claims, and argue by exhaustion of a trichotomy: (1) On the one hand, utterers cannot be free of all demands to check and eliminate counterpossibilities to their claims, because the claims would then be without value for conveying information. As we have seen, even setting aside skeptical doubts, where anything goes in this way there would be guaranteed to be virtually no point in making assertions, because they would just amount to pure guesses. (2) On the other hand, if utterers are held to a perfect standard and are required to eliminate all counterpossibilities, including "Cartesian" ones that are presently regarded as extraordinarily unlikely, no one can ever actually make a satisfactory unchallenged assertion; the Cartesian methodology entails skeptical paralysis. After all, to err is human. The whole assertion-making enterprise thus becomes unusable and again worthless. (3) Hence, the only possibly useful option is a standard of some, but not perfect, care, as in the special reasons requirement.

The "transcendental" conclusion here is merely that, given the communal value of an information-conveying procedure, the standard of care in counterpossibility-checking below which the agent is criticized as negligent must fall between perfection and utter leniency. In any community without such an intermediate standard of moderate care, the activity of making assertions must be virtually valueless. It should be noted again that I am setting aside skepticism in the present discussion. (Of course, one can wonder whether a standard that eliminates some counterpossibilities yields more confidence or warrant than no standard at all, and even whether justification procedures that eliminate "relevant" or apparently more likely possibilities are more likely to yield truths than a procedure that just eliminates counterpossibilities at random. The inference from a claim's not being subject to criticism in the above way to its being warranted will be examined in section 5.8.)[2]

Even in the one-person case, it is important for a man on a desert island—indeed, also for each member of a society—to be able to trust in the above way the reliability of his own earlier conclusions without having always to reconstruct and evaluate his reasoning to those conclusions. The individual must in effect be able to communicate forward in time with himself in order for his own knowledge to be cumulative, that is, for him to be able to build upon his own earlier conclusions. Furthermore, the usefulness even of primitive nonlinguistic communication requires a community whose members can rely on each other to eliminate some, if not all, counterpossibilities—namely, common false alarms for emitting a signal. In this way, innate pigeon warning wing-flicking motions in response to passing helicopters—rather than, for example, hawks—have made these signals worse than worthless for flocks in areas with high air traffic and low predator populations.

We saw earlier that common-law standards of reasonable care include "fine structure" provisions that higher standards are applied when the agent has greater mental capacity or expertise and when a bad outcome would have more serious consequences. Some "ought implies can" rationale can now be offered for setting the level of care on the basis of the agent's ability and knowledge; there is no point in requiring a given class of agents to do what is impossible for them—in particular, to anticipate possibilities that they cannot foresee. Similarly, since checking counterpossibilities has a cognitive cost, the smaller the perceived probability or size of risk involved in an act, the less care is justified as a cost-benefit trade-off, other things being equal.

Such considerations suggest a rough typology of multiple standards. The diverging goals, risks, and available resources in everyday life, law, scientific inquiry, and philosophy dictate different levels of care in checking counterpossibilities to knowledge claims. In everyday situations we do not have the time to act on opportunities that is available in careful experimentation, hence "quicker but dirtier" commonsense procedures ought to be employed; precautions appropriate for science would often be unreasonably elaborate in ordinary life. Again, in law there are appropriately higher standards of evidence than in ordinary life—for instance, excluding hearsay testimony—since, typically, much more is at stake. And in the theory of knowledge the goal is not necessarily procedures that are usable in everyday life. Even Descartes argues, by the end of the first *Meditation,* that his method of doubt is not overdone—for instance, because of the dream possibility—since "I am not now considering the question of action, but only of knowledge" (1955b, 148). At least in this way, one can understand why Descartes might have therefore suspended any everyday requirement of special reasons for raising a counterpossibility.

5.3 Pragmatism and Neopragmatism

The special reasons requirement turns out to fit particularly well with pragmatist epistemologies. This connection is not surprising when one considers that C. S. Peirce's position when he founded American pragmatism could be characterized as beginning with across-the-board rejection of what he viewed as the Cartesian methodology. The central doctrine of Peirce's reaction against Descartes was "critical commonsensism." Its first thesis—of "commonsensism"—rejects universal doubt:

We cannot begin with complete doubt. We must begin with all the prejudices which we actually have when we enter upon the study of philosophy. These prejudices are not to be dispelled by a maxim, for they are things which it does not occur to us *can* be questioned. (1932, 5.265)

The second thesis—of "fallibilism"—rejects as impossible perfectionism the Cartesian goal of indubitable, absolutely certain axioms for knowledge:

An inquiry, to have that completely satisfactory result called demonstration, has only to start with propositions perfectly free from all actual doubt. If the premises are not in fact doubted at all, they cannot be more satisfactory than they are. (1932, 5.358)[3]

Peirce's sentiments here of course sound familiar to readers of Quine's *Word and Object*. Quine chose as the book's epigraph and *leitmotif* a now-famous quotation from Neurath's "Protokolsätze": in translation, "We are like sailors who must rebuild their ship on the open sea, never able to dismantle it in drydock and to reconstruct it there out of the best materials" (1959, 201). The boat is the conceptual scheme that philosophers find they have already been accepting when they first begin epistemological inquiry. Peirce and Neurath agree that we must, by and large, accept our current scheme. They seem to diverge, however, in their reasons why we must do so. Peirce says that we are psychologically unable to doubt at will as Descartes demands, just as we cannot arbitrarily decide to believe something. "Doubting is not as easy as lying"; real, sincere doubt is painful. We therefore "acritically" take for granted most of the scheme as background.

Neurath's image, however, suggests instead that we cannot undertake Descartes's method of universal doubt because if we try, we are sunk; we drown. That is clearly the moral Quine draws in chapter 1 of *Word and Object*: if seriously practiced, the Cartesian method must leave us in the tragicomic cognitive paralysis that seems to be history's majority verdict upon the last five *Meditations*. Beginning with so blank a slate would entail a kind of virtual self-lobotomy. The Quinian position that Cartesian doubt is in this way unfeasible should be distinguished from the antiskeptical conclusion Quine goes on to draw from the Neurath's boat point, namely, that we cannot even meaningfully ask about the correctness of our total scheme. (On this distinction, see chapter 6.) The present chapter proceeds on the assumption that one can accept the Neurath's boat point without Quine's further conclusion.

What is the relation of the special reasons requirement to critical commonsensism and its inheritors? In "Some Consequences of Four Incapacities" Peirce says,

A person may, . . . in the course of his studies, find reason to doubt what he began by believing; but in that case he doubts because he has a positive reason for it, and not on account of the Cartesian maxim. (1932, 5.265)

Peirce's claim corresponds to Austin's point that an utterer's assertion that a goldfinch is in the garden can only be challenged if the challenger has "some concrete reason" to suppose the utterer may be mistaken in this case. That is, when Peirce (or Neurath or Quine) (1) asserts that we must at any given time take for granted the majority of our beliefs and (2) rejects Cartesian perfectionism for the thesis that no belief is absolutely immune to doubt and any single belief by itself can be questioned and subjected to test; (3) the special reasons requirement identifies *when* challenge of a belief *is* legitimate. We are in a position to doubt, rather than believe, only when there is a definite specific basis to do so.

5.4 Psychologistic versus Absolute Requirements

The role of the special reasons requirement in the knowledge-gathering process is therefore to "filter" the challenges the agent is responsible for checking and eliminating. How does this counterpossibility filter operate? One important type of answer is straightforwardly psychologistic (or "internalist"): 'The agent is responsible for all and only those counterpossibilities that occur to him, that he happens to be thinking about at the time he makes his claim'. Some signs of this view appear in Austin: for example, "If you say 'That's not enough,' then you must have in mind some more or less definite lack" (1979, 84). Alvin Goldman seems to have arrived independently of Austin at a special reasons requirement of his own in early versions of his causal analysis of knowledge, as in "Discrimination and Perceptual Knowledge" (1976, especially pp. 775–778). Goldman describes himself as "attracted by," although "officially neutral" toward, similarly subjectivistic views of what are the "relevant possibilities" an agent must be able to distinguish according to his account of knowledge. For example, Goldman seems to suggest that this type of relevance should be affected by the fact that "If the speaker is in a class where Descartes's evil demon has just been discussed, . . . he may think of alternatives he would not otherwise think of and will perhaps treat them seriously" (1976, 776).

But at least this simple type of procedure for determining relevant counterpossibilities seems both too stringent and too lenient. The procedure is too strong: If I have just seen the science fiction movie *Attack of the Killer Tomatoes,* my wondering that evening about the safety of my salad is understandable, but it is not on only this basis justifiable or appropriate. In this situation, when I asserted, 'Here is the salad', my considering the dangerous quasi-tomato possibility would be explainable, but nonetheless a joke, not an obligation. A psychologistic requirement of special reasons also seems too weak: As was clear in the earlier discussion of tort law, carelessly failing to think of counterpossibilities to a claim of, say, an automobile's safety does not by itself reduce responsibility for eliminating those counterpossibilities. The psychologistic requirement is unsatisfactory because it implies that, in some ways, the more careful the agent is in thinking of counterpossibilities, the less he is entitled to claim to know; and the sloppier he is, the more he is entitled to assert. The requirement is inadequate because, whatever the mysteries of deriving epistemic 'ought' from 'is', it turns actual human behavior, whatever it might be, too directly into norms; it ends up really bypassing the idea of "playing by the rules of the knowledge-gathering (or belief-forming) game." The psychologistic requirement is not in fact our special reasons requirement; furthermore, it would not be a good design for a special reasons requirement in terms of the "division of cognitive labor" rationale discussed earlier.

At the other extreme would be an "absolute" (or externalist) requirement: 'The agent is responsible for those counterpossibilities that in fact are fairly likely'. An agent's claim is thus to be evaluated as if he were "partially omniscient," having perfect information about facts regarding the plausibility of counterexamples to the claim. In *Knowledge and the Flow of Information* Fred Dretske (1981, especially pp. 123–134) proposed, in what we can now see as a rather Austinian vein, that "To know, or to have received information, is to have eliminated *all relevant alternative possibilities*" to what is supposed to be known (p. 133). On the one hand, Dretske concludes his discussion of his special reasons requirement by saying that how we apply a concept like "relevant alternative possibility" to concrete situations is relative to, for instance, what beliefs we take for granted (pp.

132–133). But on the other hand, most of his earlier discussion is of this tenor:

> To qualify as a relevant possibility, one that actually affects the equivocation of (and therefore information in) a signal, the possibility envisaged must actually be realizable in the nuts and bolts of the particular system in question. If, in the past, signals of kind R have arrived when s was not F (whether or not this is known is immaterial), that settles the matter. . . . Signals of kind R are equivocal with respect to s's being F . . . (p. 131)

Whether these assertions of both the relativity and the absoluteness of knowledge can be reconciled, as Dretske seems to claim, is not my concern here. I am seeking not conditions necessary for actual knowledge, but only assertability conditions: ones that must be satisfied for an agent properly to make a claim, or a knowledge claim—in other words, for him not to be subject to criticism as negligent if the assertion turns out to have been wrong. In fact, not fully distinguishing between conditions for genuine knowledge (in particular, *true* justified belief) and for just assertability may be why signs of both the absolute special reasons requirement and the earlier psychologistic one tend to appear together in discussions of the notion of relevance.

As a condition on assertability, the absolute special reasons requirement seems again, like the psychologistic requirement, both too stringent and too lenient. It is too strong: Subject to provisos discussed below, if I (and my present audience) cannot be expected to know that many neighborhood children have in fact been playing lately with toy goldfinches, it is not appropriate for the audience to criticize my claim 'A goldfinch is in the garden' by pointing out that I have not considered whether it might actually be a toy. In real everyday conversation in this situation, the counterpossibility would be just a joke, even though a joke that turned out accidentally to apply. (Such an absolute special reasons requirement on knowledge seems immediately in danger of implying that agents can never know that they know a proposition, since they can never have perfect information about which counterpossibilities really are likely.) As we saw earlier in the discussion of negligence law, 'ought' must imply 'can' here, in that there is little point in demanding an absolutely unattainable standard of care of the agent; "reasonable care" in making assertions therefore does not, and ought not to, require omniscience. To some extent, we must put outselves in the agent's shoes.

In addition, the absolute requirement manages to be too weak: If the agent and his community have good reason to believe that a counterpossibility—for instance, to his claim of the safety of his automobile's brakes—is genuine, then he is held responsible for checking it even if in fact it is very unlikely. After all, how can the agent or his hearers possibly know this? They cannot evaluate counterpossibilities by magic. In this way, contrary to Dretske, the agent in this case can fail to *know* the brakes are safe. A God's-eye perspective seems to exonerate too much.

5.5 Minimal Requirements

What requirement of reasonable care can avoid the problems of both the psychologistic and the absolute conditions? One middle-ground requirement would be 'The agent is responsible for all and only those counterpossibilities whose seriousness is implied by the agent's current belief set'. The counterpossibilities that must be considered are "*apparently* relevant" ones, with relevance relativized to the agent's present beliefs, rather than defined in terms of a perspective of perfect information. Nonetheless, the agent is not just responsible for the counterpossibilities that happen to occur to him; unrecalled background information can raise possibilities, as well as eliminate them. The role of the agent's total belief system in eliminating "idle" counterpossibilities from consideration is thus a special case of Quine's generalization in "Two Dogmas of Empiricism" of the Duhemian thesis, that a very broad range of background belief must inevitably be appealed to in experimentally testing any proposition. Part of the holistic character of empirical test and justification is just that remotely related background information is tacitly involved in excluding counterpossibilities.

This special reasons requirement improves on earlier ones, but it is still too stringent. There are, of course, an infinite number of inferences in first-order logic, each of which would take a normal human being more than a life span to perform; in addition, there is a set of similarly intractable inductive inferences. Cases are easy to envisage where such an unfeasible inference from the agent's belief set is required to reveal the seriousness of a counterpossibility. Given some "ought implies can" rationale here, a requirement of reasonable care cannot demand an ideal agent who in effect must be able to maintain deductive closure of his belief set. The requirement instead must employ a "golden mean" notion of a minimal agent who must have some, but not perfect, inferential competence.

A better approximation of a minimal requirement of special reasons therefore is

The agent is responsible for some, but not all, counterpossibilities whose seriousness is implied by his current belief set.

Now, *which* deductive inferences is the agent responsible for making? In chapter 1 I argued that the inferential competence that is a sine qua non for a creature to qualify as an agent at all is a proper subset of minimal normative rationality, the nonidealized standard that the agent ought to meet and that, if he does not, leaves him open to criticism. The key point is that the minimal special reasons requirement seems to hold the agent to some normative rationality standard, such that the agent can fail to meet this higher standard in his selection of counterpossibilities without thereby failing to qualify even as a minimal agent.

Some of the fine structure of this middle standard of normative rationality is provided by the commonsense cognitive psychology that seems shared at least by members of typical human cultures (indeed, much of it may in fact be innate predisposition). As was evident in the earlier discussion of common law, we have a psychological model of the competencies of the "reasonable man" In chapter 2 I argued that, in predicting and explaining behavior, we seem to use a pretheoretical profile of normal deductive competence, in particular, of the relative difficulty of different deductive inferences. Correspondingly, any typical agent is more liable to a charge of negligence for failing to make an obvious *modus tollens* inference to the conclusion that a counterpossibility is serious, than for failing to make some tricky quantification-theoretic inference to a similar conclusion. We also seem to have a theory of the typical feasibility of nondeductive inferences. (However, many of the recent studies of the formal incorrectness of everyday quick and dirty reasoning heuristics suggest that some of the commonsense model of nondeductive competence may itself be rather unrealistically idealized. For a review of this work, see Nisbett and Ross 1980.)

Our commonsense model of the cognitive psychology of the reasonable man also includes a "module" dealing with the structure and capabilities of the agent's memory. As discussed in chapter 3, we predict and explain much human behavior (particularly involving making "obvious" mistakes) in terms of a duplex model: at any moment, most of a person's beliefs are in a long-term memory where they cannot affect the choice of actions; only beliefs in the quite limited-capacity short-term working memory can be premises of the person's inferences. I argued that, consequently, an agent can achieve required minimal inferential competence only if he has some (but, of course, not perfect) capacity to recall from long-term to working memory the presently relevant beliefs. Similarly, an agent's satisfaction of the minimal special reasons requirement here in turn requires some recall efficiency in bringing to mind background beliefs needed to identify currently relevant counterpossibilities. And again, we seem to have some idea of the relative difficulty of different recall tasks; agents often are not held to be negligent when they fail at difficult memory tasks that only a mnemonist could be expected to perform.

5.6 Heuristic Imbeciles

Clearly, satisfying the minimal special reasons requirement can only be a necessary, not a sufficient, condition for competence in identifying relevant counterpossibilities. Most important, the agent must also satisfy an "input" requirement: 'The agent must collect, and remember, enough available information'. An agent can be criticized as not exercising reasonable care for failing to acquire the background beliefs needed to evaluate a current counterpossibility. What is "available information"? When I claim a goldfinch is in the garden without checking whether it might be stuffed, and it turns out later that it is stuffed and that many neighborhood children have been playing with such toys recently, I might plead in my defense that I did not know the children had been playing with stuffed birds; but a rebuttal might be that I ought to have *noticed* the children's new fad, since it was so widespread, and therefore checked whether the putative bird in the garden was stuffed. In some cases "ignorance is no excuse"; the test is "what I knew or *should* have known." Like the above requirements, this input requirement is minimal, in that it can only demand reasonable care, that is, that the agent collect some of the more easily available current information, rather than all of it.

In fact, the counterpossibilities that must be considered are relative not to the solitary agent's own background knowledge but to the shared knowledge of the appropriate community. Part of the social character of the knowledge-gathering process discussed earlier is that the agent is held responsible for counterpossibilities his community has recognized as serious. For example, the judged likelihood of a potential loss affects the legal standard of reasonable care; such estimates (for instance, of the probability of a particular type of automobile brake malfunction) often are based on assumptions of community-wide agreement, rather than only on the individual's possibly idiosyncratic judgment. Doctrines like "Ignorance of the law is no excuse" indicate that the agent is held to a standard of care that includes responsibility for collecting information by consulting appropriate experts in the community. The community in question can be quite volatile, consisting of the speaker and his current audience, as when Austin points out that "precautions cannot be more than reasonable, relative to current intents and purposes" (1979, 88). Speaker and audience are assumed to share certain purposes and background. Therefore, contrary to an egocentric or even ethnocentric perspective, the typical agent seems to be included in a changing hierarchy of overlapping knowledge-gathering communities. (Just how the relevant community is determined in a given case will not be pursued here.)

Since a real agent cannot collect all interesting information, if he is to be moderately competent at identifying relevant counterpossibilities, he must to some extent know where to look for the apparently most useful information. That is, a necessary condition for satisfying the input requirement is having some empirical inquiry-selecting ability. I have argued that an agent must have some deductive inquiry-selecting ability; a putative agent who chose deductive tasks at random would squander his cognitive resources and so be deductively paralyzed, hence in fact not an agent at all. In addition, I argued that agents with anything like a human duplex memory structure must also have some ability to choose which items seem most useful to recall from "cold storage" to working memory, or else be similarly paralyzed. Thus, the empirical inquiry-selecting ability required of a competent counterpossibility-identifier is not ad hoc, but a special case of a fundamental ability to select appropriate inquiries. At least some parts of that ability are required for rationality; heuristic imbeciles cannot be agents.

One can argue, as I have, that an entity must possess some deductive inference capacity in order to qualify as an agent. However, at least the full-blooded typical human set of nondeductive reasoning abilities does not seem as central to rational agenthood (although some of it still seems more than a mere low-level empirical generalization about *Homo sapiens*). That is, one can make sense of various sorts of inductive, as opposed to deductive, imbeciles that still possess recognizable systems of beliefs and desires, or at least something that seems a borderline case of such a cognitive system. For instance, a pocket computer video game is at most a degenerate special case of an agent; it has no moral rights or responsibilities, and its "empirical" contact with the external world is no more than direct keystroke entry. Nonetheless, we make sense of, and predict, its behavior by supposing that it has a chief goal—to win—and at least internal representations of the current state of the game, long-range and short-range strategies, and so on.[4]

I have argued thus far for the following main points:

1. Normal human beings are subject to normative standards of nondeductive competence; in particular, they are held responsible, and subject to criticism as negligent, if they do not eliminate some apparently relevant counterpossibilities to their claims.

2. There is a "transcendental rationale" for including such a special reasons requirement in the pragmatics of virtually any interesting type of linguistic community.

3. Furthermore, nothing finite could qualify at all as any type of rational agent if it did not possess some nondeductive competencies, in particular, the key heuristic ability to select apparently useful deductive tasks (and, for agents with large-scale duplex memories, a corresponding limited-search recall ability).

4. In addition, part of our commonsense cognitive psychology includes the expectation that normal adult human beings *in fact* will have a full profile of nondeductive competencies, including

an ability to identify some apparently relevant counterpossibilities. We assume that people conform to at least the broad outlines of a typical feasibility ordering for nondeductive inferences, just as we assume they do for deductive inferences.

5. Nevertheless, it seems no more than a matter of nomenclature whether something that is unable to satisfy the special reasons requirement (but is, for instance, minimally deductively competent) is still said to have a belief-desire system.

5.7 Inquiry Selection

How can an epistemic agent decide whether a line of inquiry is likely to be one of the currently apparently more useful ones—in particular, without having in the process already accomplished the inquiry? An *Encyclopedia of Ignorance* seems conceptually a somewhat tricky enterprise.[5] This "20/20 foresight" problem has a structure similar to the dilemma of inquiry that Plato introduces in the *Meno:* "A man cannot inquire either about that which he knows, or about that which he does not know; for if he knows, he has no need to inquire; and if not, he cannot; for he does not know the very subject about which he is to inquire" (1937, 80). In the latter case, "If you find what you want, how will you ever know that this is the thing which you did not know?" That is, how can we recognize what we do not know, much less know what we ought to try to find out, without thereby already having come to know it? The solution to both problems seems to lie in the hypothesis that the agent has prior partial knowledge. Plato's reply in the rest of the *Meno* to his paradox is his doctrine of recollection, that people can recognize the correct answers to their questions (at least concerning a priori knowledge) because they already have some inborn ("confused") knowledge about what would constitute a right answer.

Correspondingly, many basic and useful human information-collecting strategies have simply been hard-wired by natural selection. For example, a hierarchy of attentional mechanisms governs all vertebrate vision. The very structure of the human visual field embodies such strategies (see, for instance, Cornsweet 1970). The periphery of the field detects motion rather than fine detail; only the small central retinal area (the fovea) serves the computationally costly processes of high-resolution perception. However, visual system reflexes immediately orient the central field of the eye toward motion detected by the periphery; the visual system thus embodies the assumption that what moves in certain ways is more likely to be interesting than what does not. A similar rationale is apparent in the "startle reflex" to orient toward a loud noise. Generally, perceptual systems are tuned to detect change; "boredom" so broadly conceived is the ultimate information-selecting strategy. Of course, such innate procedures cannot always succeed in gathering the most important information (to some extent, they are cognitive fossils of our evolutionary past), but the strategies do not have to be perfect for the minimal competencies described above; educated guesses that are better than random gambles can suffice. Many layers of learned routines (the "education of attention") and of conscious decisions can supplement the innate information-selection processes—for instance, in deciding which hundred-million-dollar particle physics research project is most worthy of funding in light of current knowledge.

Since each such decision itself involves a more or less advisable inquiry, a regress of heuristic decisions threatens. The important point here is that the above plausible evolutionary innateness hypothesis seems to stop that regress by postulating that some basic strategies are built in. The hypothesis also seems to explain how particular processes of counterpossibility elimination can be feasible in another respect: no agent could actually consider the infinite number of counterpossibilities to any claim, much less then exclude from further examination the irrelevant ones. The above discussion suggests that evolution has simply constructed our heuristic preprocessing procedures so that we will ordinarily never even try to consider most of these possibilities; we literally unthinkingly take their irrelevance for granted.[6] Such innateness hypotheses also help explain how human infants avoid a bootstrap problem at the beginning of their empirical knowledge-gathering career. An initially "tabula rasa" epistemic agent would only be able to acquire sound (uncriticizable) empirical beliefs by use of his "relevance filter" on counterpossibilities, yet at start-up the filter would not be able to operate because none of the requisite background beliefs could then be present. In contrast, an appropriately innately equipped neonate can begin accumulating beliefs until he attains the critical mass of background beliefs needed for relevance filtering.

5.8 Breakdowns

A description of the structure of the counterpossibility-elimination procedure must include a delimitation of its scope. To begin, let us glance at the large question of whether Austin's special reasons requirement really can succeed, as it seems to have been intended, in eliminating even a few of the traditional Cartesian counterpossibilities to knowledge. For example, could any agent have background beliefs that would suffice to exclude from consideration the skeptical possibility that he might be the victim all along of a hallucination that was perfectly indistinguishable from experience of an independently existing external world? Of course, our system of background assumptions typically includes premises for the conclusion that such a hallucination is extremely unlikely. But one can now wonder whether these background beliefs are not in turn completely susceptible to second-order skeptical worries.

A familiar unstoppable regress of required counterpossibility exclusions now threatens again to render most important knowledge claims subject to criticism. Our hard-wired perceptual strategies and so on discussed earlier in fact end actual consideration of the regress of counterpossibility-elimination procedures; but that does not in itself show that those strategies *ought* to terminate the regress of challenges. For one can then put Mother Nature on the stand: Why must She always be right? That is, why should the evolutionarily selected exclusion of possibilities be warranted (for example, why should it be at all more likely to yield truths), as opposed to merely efficient for information processing and terrestrial survival? (For more on doubts about the normative conclusions to be drawn from naturalizing epistemology, see chapter 6.) When Hume pointed out that it is part of human nature to ignore skeptical doubts, he did not conclude that he thereby disproved skepticism.

Of course, classical ordinary language philosophy, and Austin in particular, have long been charged with excessive conservatism; Austin (1979) takes for granted that the actual is the ideal, that the "established," "recognized" procedures for distinguishing dreaming and waking must always be adequate (see pp. 87, 112, 182). But even pragmatism and its inheritors, with their focus on the progress of science, will have similar difficulties with the epistemological status of background assumptions involved in evaluating counterpossibilities.

Peirce's anti-Cartesian fallibilism asserted that no beliefs were immune to reasonable challenge; but such a view does not seem true to the Carnapian (1956) and Kuhnian (1970) insight that not all assumptions are equal, that fundamental framework principles in fact seem harder to reject "rationally" than smaller-scale "internal" scientific theory. For example, when Quine asserts that any statement in the web of belief can be rejected, it is natural to shift Quinian metaphors and wonder about ripping out planks below the waterline of Neurath's boat. From the perspective of our present boat, how can we coherently envisage rejection, however gradual, of principles so basic that they must be employed in *any* argument? (Similarly, how could such planks be rationally acquired during ontogenetic or scientific development in the first place?) Peircean and Quinian epistemologies do not account well for the most important type of scienfic progress, radical revision of fundamental "standard procedures"—devising the game, as opposed to playing it. Quine seems forced to end up about as conservative as Austin for central elements of a conceptual system, which will include major portions of the counterpossibility-elimination apparatus.

In addition, the counterpossibility-evaluation procedures seem especially more prone to faltering, the more limited the relevant background belief set. In particular, the more a situation is perceived as unprecedented, the more hesitant the agent is forced to be in eliminating possibilities as unlikely. Even with Cartesian skepticism resolutely set aside, such anything-goes conditions are intrinsic to state-of-the-art inquiry. (Indeed, given that such inquiry is hampered in this way, an explanation is needed for the puzzle of how it can successfully proceed at all.) These wide-open contexts are not peculiar to exotic scientific research; every child's cognitive development involves a similar type of cutting edge of knowledge, where incomplete mastery of new domains ensures unpredictability. In these areas what counts as "reasonable care" just cannot be well defined. Another important group of such "Twilight Zone" cases concerns evaluation of the impact of new technologies on public policy. For example, what are legitimate disaster scenarios to review is a matter of much presently inconclusive debate in determining the acceptable level of risk of unprecedented consequences from environmental carcinogens, nuclear power plants, and nuclear weapons. (A U.S. Air Force major reportedly was discharged recently for asking, during underground silo missile launch training, "If I get an order to fire, how can I be sure it's real?" (*Mother Jones Magazine*, Sept./Oct. 1982, 10).) The counterpossibility-elimination procedure is therefore inescapably limited by the necessarily incomplete state of a finite agent's knowledge at any given moment.

This chapter has sketched a portion of our total empirical knowledge-gathering system, namely, the procedures by which we determine whether a counterpossibility to a knowledge claim ought to be dealt with. The requirement of special reasons for considering a counterpossibility has a minimal rationality structure; that is, some but not all possibilities must be eliminated. A special reasons requirement can be found in pragmatist and neopragmatist anti-Cartesianism. The requirement also turns out closely to resemble legal standards of reasonable but not perfect care for actions in general. Some historical and cross-cultural evidence suggests the requirement is a type of societal universal, not just an idiosyncrasy of Anglo-American tradition. And in fact, a conditional "transcendental" rationale can be given for it: Given some antiskeptical assumptions, a special reasons requirement, rather than utter leniency or Cartesian perfectionism, seems indispensable for interesting language use.

To avoid the difficulties of psychologistic and absolute formulations, the requirement must at least be stated as 'The agent is responsible for some but not all counterpossibilities whose seriousness is implied by his current beliefs'. Because of the key role of background beliefs, there is an additional minimal "input" requirement: The agent is responsible for acquiring some of the beliefs relevant to evaluating counterpossibilities. To satisfy this input requirement without regress, the agent in turn must at least have some innate inquiry-selecting strategies. Finally, although the special reasons requirement can be expected to work well in familiar domains, breakdowns are inevitable so long as an agent's knowledge system has a cutting edge; that is, they are inevitable *simpliciter*.

6

Limits for Knowledge

In this final chapter I turn to the traditional problem in the theory of knowledge concerning skepticism about, for instance, the belief that there is an external world. For various reasons, including the intractability of this problem, a number of philosophers, notably Quine, have proposed a reorientation of the theory of knowledge, the "naturalization" of epistemology. Such a naturalized epistemology is conceived of as a basic element of a complete empirical cognitive science; it takes for granted that we do know there is an external world, and examines our actual knowledge-gathering procedures—for example, the input-output relation between a subject's sensory history and the total conceptual scheme he constructs (see Quine 1969a). Such a descriptive enterprise is undeniably of value (indeed, the task of the previous chapter was of this kind). The question is, Can a naturalized epistemology coherently avoid the traditional challenges of the adequacy of our knowledge-gathering practices? I will argue that the program of naturalizing epistemology entails, in effect, a kind of antinomy: even as it sets aside traditional skepticism, it provides the basis for a new conclusion that there are philosophically significant limits for empirical knowledge. Our knowledge would be limited in this way in all but the most implausibly manageable of possible worlds.

Symptoms of this tension appear in earlier attempts to eliminate the philosophical question of how well reality fits the "ideal theory." For example, Peirce's classical attempt directly to define away the question is "The opinion which is fated to be ultimately agreed to by all who investigate, is what we mean by the truth" (1932, 5.407). Yet, only two pages earlier, Peirce also endorses a conception of mind-independent reality that his own definition of truth seems prima facie to exclude: "We may define the real as that whose characters are independent of what anybody may think them to be" (5.405). How can Peirce have reality so mind-independent—"entirely independent of our opinions"—if truth is not, if "any man, if he have sufficient experience and he reason enough about it, will be led to the one True conclusion"? (5.384). Although the distinction here between subjective and objective conceptions of reality remains in need of much clarification, it is interesting to find signs of a parallel ambivalence between Putnam's (1978, 1981) recent arguments for "internal" (as opposed to "metaphysical") realism and his Pickwickian implication that internal realism is not in fact entirely antirealist.

Part of the philosophical import of the knowledge limitations I shall describe is that they suggest that verificationism fails in one of its principal functions in philosophy: to eliminate the distinction between appearance (our current or ideal theories) and mind-independent reality, by making skepticism cognitively meaningless. Nonetheless, despite its failings, some moderate verificationism is extremely difficult to avoid; we must acknowledge a *pressure* toward it. For present purposes, verificationism can be identified with the following version of the verifiability principle: 'If proposition p is cognitively meaningful, then it is logically possible to confirm or disconfirm p.' 'Cognitively meaningful' here means 'capable of being true or false' (see, for example, Schlick 1959a).

6.1 Neurath's Boat

Let us start, at the beginning of the post-logical positivist era, with Quine's argument,

We cannot detach ourselves from [our conceptual scheme] and compare it objectively with an unconceptualized reality. Hence it is meaningless, I suggest, to inquire into the absolute correctness of a conceptual scheme as a mirror of reality. (1961b, 79)

This "Neurath's boat" argument recurs, of course, a decade later in *Word and Object*, with the same premise, "There is no such cosmic exile," and the same conclusion (1960, 275). And another two decades later, in *Theories and Things*, Quine argues in the same way to the same conclusion, that "What evaporates is the transcendental question of the reality of the external world—the question whether or in how far our science measures up to the *Ding an sich*" (1981, 22). Quine's argument is very strong: we cannot ask about correctness of our *current* total theory, much less a Peirceanly ideal one. Is Quine committed to the extreme view that we cannot regard even our present theory as fallible and incomplete? Of course, Quine is just as well known for insisting to the contrary, for instance, in the lines preceding the first quotation of this section, "We can improve our conceptual scheme . . . bit by bit while continuing to depend on it for support." However, as with Peirce, there seems to be a tension between these two Quinian views: I will argue that the Quinian program of naturalizing epistemology and the account of charity of translation are indeed cases where Quine excludes the possibility of at least large-scale errors or gaps in our current conceptual scheme.

Furthermore, I will argue that even the epistemic idealizations of verificationism clash with one of the most basic elements of our total theory, our picture of man's place in nature. The scientific world view has relatively unexplored implications that conflict with the secular credo of a Peircean, American epistemological optimism—that "Nature cannot fool all of the investigators all of the time," that is, forever. (Competition of ideas in the free marketplace of inquiry must yield indefinite perfectibility of man's knowledge, and so on.) The opposing view is a challenge of scientific methodology's guarantee of total truth, and not just a claim that this truth can only be approximate: it is deeply implausible that man can have a complete and completely correct theory of the universe. Science may be the final arbiter of truth, and science itself may explain its own success (for instance, as Richard Boyd has proposed that a realist causal theory of perception accounts for the convergence of mature theory); but it also suggests limits for this success.

Indeed, our world view seems schizoid, in that it includes both the above scientistic, Peircean optimism and conflicting platitudes of pessimism. The basic idea of the following sort of limits for knowledge is therefore not new. For example, versions of the first argument below seem to be at least as old as the theory of evolution. Elements of the argument appear in Bergson's *Creative Evolution* (1911); Du Bois-Reymond's (1872) assertion, "Ignoramus et ignorabimus" ("We are ignorant and shall remain ignorant" on some scientific matters), was rejected by Hilbert (1935) in his famous "Mathematical Problems" paper (subsequent incompleteness results of course have constrained Hilbertian optimism for mathematical knowledge).

6.2 Occam's Razor

My two arguments can be thought of as attempting a kind of cognitive jujitsu, so that naturalized epistemology ends up undercutting itself. The arguments gain force from a Great Chain of Being perspective that is also part of the scientific world view. The naturalistic standpoint reveals a hierarchy of organisms more primitive than ourselves. From our position of relative omniscience, we know on the phylogenetic scale that flies can never understand fly bottles, cats cannot figure out canary recordings, and so on. Even without our own species the chain of levels of cognitive capacity continues in our theories of ontogenetic development of children, comparative cultural anthropology, and the history of our own science. It is then natural to extrapolate from this "downward-looking" viewpoint to the idea that some puzzles may be intractable for us, too. We cannot emerge from our own Platonic cave.

The first argument for limits of knowledge is that the conceptual scheme we possess is the result of our use of methodological principles, in particular, Occam's Razor; but it seems *to us* somewhat more likely than not that what we judge to be the simplest—or most natural, plausible, elegant, or useful— theory will not always be the correct one. The point goes beyond just speculating about whether we have the slightest good reason to expect that the world really is objectively simple—for instance, whether Occam's Razor can be noncircularly justified. For example, Donald Campbell (and even Quine) points out that natural selection builds into us particular perceptual and cognitive biases (see Campbell 1974 and, on our innate sense of similarity, Quine 1969b). But why should what is innate be *true*, as opposed to just efficient or conducive to species survival? For whether or not the world is "objectively simple" in any sense, we have to accept simpler theories, other things being equal, for the "subjective" reason that otherwise our limited minds would eventually be overwhelmed by gratuitous complexity.

On the one hand, biology, psychology, anthropology, and so on, suggest that evolution designed our cognitive tool kit for a specific terrestrial hunter-gatherer environment of middle-sized objects like bananas and lions. On the other hand, physics customarily trichotomizes its objects of investigation by size into three domains. The first is the above middling one of everyday human experience, accessible to our unaided senses, where Euclidean geometry and classical mechanics apply well. The second is the astrophysical/cosmological realm of the largest objects—planets, stars, galaxies, the entire universe. Here gravity is the dominant force, and non-Euclidean geometry and general relativity theory apply best. The third domain is that of microphysics, of very small particles studied over very short intervals; nuclear forces dominate, and quantum mechanics with its nonclassical models of causation best applies. There are many other dimensions besides size on which we can similarly extrapolate in either direction—temperature, density of matter, age of the universe, duration of events. Without challenging the unity of science, we can see that on these dimensions, Uniformity or Homogeneity of Nature does not seem to hold too strictly.

From this "*Scientific American*" perspective (see, for example, Morrison and Morrison 1981), the universe appears to have a nested structure: we seem to be able to extrapolate indefinitely on many of these scales. The plausibility of the cosmological hypothesis that the universe is virtually unlimited in diversity therefore seems at least an interestingly open empirical question. And the normal human terrestrial environment falls in the middle here in many ways. The history of our science and culture of course indicates that, as our theories and instrument technology develop, our investigations are taking us farther and farther from the original middle-sized domain, into, for example, the clearly very different astrophysical and microphysical realms. This occurs much too rapidly for natural selection to keep us cognitively pretuned in any respect. We therefore face the worse than Sisyphean prospect that, as we master familiar domains, we confront an indefinite series of stranger domains.

Must our intelligence necessarily be sufficient for all problems we could encounter? It seems a questionable article of faith that our minds, or brains, are unlimited in flexibility and adaptability. Natural selection appears to design—over-design—for maximum efficiency in the given environment. (Two cases of perceptual, as opposed to cognitive, design closely approaching theoretical limits: human hearing is sensitive to motions of the eardrum of less than one-hundredth the diameter of a hydrogen molecule; individual retinal receptors can respond to as little as half a dozen quanta of light; see, respectively, Green 1976 and Cornsweet 1970 for reviews of the classic experimentation.) It is not at all clear that there *could* be a cognitive system attuned to all aspects of the apparently unlimited diversity and complexity of the universe. But even if this were feasible, it would not seem good design to build a species' minds that way, since the evolutionary pressure is to make trade-offs for maximum efficiency in only the terrestrial environment, and so to pretune specifically to it.

Thus, a naturalized epistemology begins by setting aside the classical justificatory questions of the adequacy of our knowledge-gathering practices, but ends up providing the basis for a new suspicion that there are deep limits for our knowledge in all but the most implausibly homogeneous and manageable of possible worlds. Indeed, it would be an odd accident if our subjective canons of scientific acceptability turned out to match in all respects the objective character of the universe. Why should our cognitive capacities be adequate for all domains, any more than our respiratory capacity can serve on mountain top or ocean floor? Ten billion *Homo sapiens,* or however many hominids have ever lived, can be wrong. We wonder, From the fact that *we* have no need of a hypothesis, just what should we conclude about its falsity? Conversely, knowing that if God did not exist we would have to postulate Him should not make many more theists.

6.3 The Finitary Predicament

The conclusion of this first argument is that we are unlikely to have entirely correct and complete theories; our innate cognitive biases may cause us to accept some falsehoods and reject some truths. The conclusion of the second argument is that we may be unable to have complete theories, because some interesting true theories (as opposed to mere exhaustive enumerations, and so forth) are likely to be too complex for us to understand, or even read through. Briefly, the starting point of this argument is one of the most fundamental aspects of the human condition, that we are in the finitary predicament of having fixed finite limits on our cognitive resources. If this thesis is part of the complete cognitive science that includes naturalized epistemology, it must be the most basic law of cognitive science, besides some principle of (moderate) maximization of utility. In contrast, our world view seems to present us with a universe of indefinitely great diversity and complexity. It does not now seem especially plausible even that the theory of the universe is finitely axiomatizable at all, much less axiomatizable in a form comprehensible to *Homo sapiens*, with no five-mile-long sentences.

Furthermore, even if all the basic laws of the universe are finitely representable, this ultimate web of belief may be unmanageable by any physically feasible agent because of fundamental information-processing limitations. It is now a familiar point that cognitive systems must exceed some minimum size, because of the holistic interdependence of beliefs, desires, and so on. In addition, I think that recent work in the field of computational complexity theory raises the possibility that there may be another "critical mass" for a knowledge representation, a maximum size threshold above which belief systems must in effect disintegrate. For a representation to qualify as being *understood* by an epistemic agent, the agent must be able to perceive an adequate proportion (of course, not necessarily all) of the interrelations among elements of the set. Otherwise, the agent will not be able to identify and eliminate enough of the inconsistencies that arise, recognize enough interesting consequences, and so on. But as the "mind's dictionary/encyclopedia" grows, it becomes much more difficult just to search, even with cataloguing and cross-referencing of its propositions or theories. In particular, the number of possible combinations among the elements explodes exponentially. Complexity theory suggests that much of this computational cost is unavoidable: many types of quite simple logical processing (for instance, just deciding validity of monadic predicate calculus sentences) are intractable—no algorithm can always evade severe combinatorial explosion.

The range of intractability results leads one to wonder in turn whether knowledge systems of some finite size may be so computationally unwieldy in this way as to shatter—perhaps to be unmanageable even by means of quick and dirty heuristics. This speculation is supported by familiar complaints about the growth, inevitability, and cost of the division of cognitive labor in the scientific community. A few hundred years ago a single person could possess all interesting scientific knowledge; today specialization is ever finer. We worry about limits to scientific, as well as economic, growth (see Price 1961, chap. 5, and Bar-Hillel 1964). Thus, there seem to be possible worlds that would be too complicated for us or a society of experts to represent feasibly, to "get it together" enough to understand. The crippling compartmentalization we in fact observe may be a symptom that ours is such a world. The breadth and depth of putatively possible knowledge may be intrinsically too great for a both manageable and complete world view, whether it is the ideal theory or just our Peircean approximations to it. For the universe may be not merely inhumanly complex, but "transcendentally" unmanageable for any physically realizable entity, for example, an ideal computer occupying the twenty billion light-year radius and twenty billion year age of the universe; the above intractability results apply with just this generality. Augmenting the human mind by means of computers should therefore not be much help.

'To be is to be comprehensible by us' thus seems implausibly and unhelpfully anthropocentric. It is wishful thinking to assume that in this sense man must be the measure of all things. That is, rejecting the above limits for knowledge requires a particular type of cosmology, one that ensures a preestablished harmony of man with universe. It would be a peculiar coincidence in need of much explanation if, for every domain, every one of the interesting true theories, and all of them together, should just happen to be simple enough to be usable by, and intelligible to, us.

6.4 Translation

The above Occam's Razor and finitary predicament arguments begin from natural questions, and there are other arguments with similar conclusions. A tension therefore emerges: Our world view contains a kind of antinomy. It implies that it itself, and presently plausible extensions of it, are unlikely to be in all respects correct and complete. We can then agree with Quine and Neurath that this world view tells us, "I'm the only scheme you've got": we cannot, and ought not to, abandon the current conceptual scheme. But its indispensability does not make it true. By what standard can it be judged?—Itself. Even if we grant that philosophy ". . . is not to be distinguished in essential points of purpose and method from good and bad science" (1960, 3–4), Quine does not thereby evade the question of the correctness (or, of course, of the completeness) of the total scheme, because our scheme *itself* suggests that the "known" (and knowable) world is not the entire actual world. And yet we do not end in Descartes's self-paralyzing universal doubt. Quine's Neurath's boat conclusion thus seems too strong—in this sense, the actual need not be the ideal.[1]

A corresponding difficulty in envisaging alternatives to, much less improvement of, the present conceptual scheme pervades Quine's account of translation. Over the same decades that Quine has espoused the Neurath's boat argument, he has claimed that to say a language is radically different from our own is

to say no more than that the translations do not come smoothly. . . . The whole truth about the most outlandish linguistic behavior is just as accessible to us, in our current Western conceptual scheme, as are other chapters of zoology. The obstacle is only that any one intercultural correlation of words and phrases, and hence of theories, will be just one among various empirically admissible correlations. . . . (1969c, 25)[2]

Thus, although Quine is of course aware of genuine conceptual revision, for instance, that engendered in set theory by Russell's Paradox, he ambivalently also holds that conceptual differences are never more than a matter of reinterpretation of utterances, of indeterminacy of translation. These claustrophobic prospects for conceptual change—no news as the only possible news—are not brightened by Quine's descriptions of the proprietors of the schemes the translator tries to interpret. The translator confronts either equals or, inevitably, "savages," "natives," "heathen," "*naturkinder*" with "jungle languages"; alternatives to our scheme are always more primitive, never more advanced. The suggestion conveyed once again is that our actual scheme must be the best.

Davidson has pressed Quine's line further, to conclude explicitly, "We have found no intelligible basis on which it can be said that schemes are different."[3] Davidson argues that, on the one hand, "failure of intertranslatability [between languages] is a necessary condition for difference of conceptual schemes" (p. 190) but that, on the other hand, by the principle of charity we cannot even count others wrong on most matters (p. 197). Thus, a dilemma: if a putative conceptual alternative is presently intelligible to us, it is just a notational variant of our own scheme and not a genuine alternative; but if it is not intelligible to us, it has not been shown to be more than gibberish. We cannot make sense of the very notion of an alternative scheme to ours, much less a better one.

The thesis of this chapter implies that this is an amazing conclusion; among other things, a "Great Chain of Being" recognition of our limited capacities and of the subjective basis of our simplicity metric makes it seem extremely unlikely that ours is the only—or ultimate—scheme.

It should be noted that a six-year-old child who had not yet mastered the concept of "prime number" could, indeed would have to, argue in this Procrustean way that grownups' talk about primes must just be noise. The argument must therefore be fallacious. In fact, it pronounces much of everyday pedagogy an impossibility. One weakness seems to be the stringency of Davidson's (and Quine's) charity principles, for example, "The basic methodological precept is . . . that a good theory of interpretation maximizes agreement" of the subject with his interpreter. We saw in section 1.5 that Davidson has even felt he had to deny that we can make sense of an agent's failure to preserve perfect preference transitivity.[4] But, to repeat a question raised for Quinian charity in chapter 4, should we be required to reinterpret Frege's *Grundgesetze*, and Quine's own *Mathematical Logic*, so that their axioms for set theory come out to be consistent?

If we demand only moderate or minimal, as opposed to perfect or near-perfect, charity, then we have the room to allow that some of a genuine scheme may not only massively disagree with ours, but be unintelligible to us. And this is no longer a mystery; we can explain it by supposing that the scheme is different from, and perhaps more sophisticated than, our own. Contrary to Davidson, the dogma of a dualism of appearance and reality consequently remains, in that we can make sense of a split between our current scheme and at least what is described by better schemes.[5]

6.5 Verificationism

An important way to reinforce the Quine-Neurath argument is by means of verificationism: challenges of the correctness of my current scheme are meaningless, because no evidence could ever bear on the issue. But now it seems that the verifiability principle similarly cannot exclude philosophically interesting limits for knowledge. Traditional skepticism says that I cannot in principle have the slightest good reason for believing (or rejecting) that, for example, there is a mind-independent reality. Since the proposition 'There is a mind-independent reality' is therefore not verifiable or falsifiable, it is cognitively meaningless according to the verifiability principle. But the conclusion of the above arguments against Quine might be called "positive skepticism": we do have a little evidence that our conceptual scheme is not correct or complete.

More important, the crucial feature is that we can envisage having more evidence that this is so; it *is* logically possible to get more confirmation of this hypothesis. We can imagine less tractable domains we might (indeed, seem likely to) encounter as we extend our investigations further and further from the ordinary terrestrial environment. For such a domain, we might find that we could construct no interesting successful theory. We know of no reason why this impasse might not persist even to an ideal limit of inquiry. The longer this cul de sac scenario continued, the more justifiable would be our loss of faith in the hypotheses either that all is knowable or that there is anything to know here—that is, that in all respects the universe is orderly. We would have to choose between the explanations that some objective regularities are inaccessible to us and that this domain is just intrinsically irregular. Other things being equal, the latter account entails more unsatisfactory—that is, unexplained—assumptions of goodness of fit between our intellects and the universe, as discussed earlier.

In at least one respect, the impossibility of knowledge suggested by the above Occam's Razor argument may be sufficiently close to traditional skepticism to be unproblematic. Even ideal inquirers with all the data there ever could be would seem to need a simplicity/plausibility metric; hence, they could still wonder whether they would be even in principle able to eliminate that source of bias. But a natural reply to the finitary predicament argument is that the alleged unknowability is merely practical and so should be ignored: it may be presently technically or even physically impossible to verify some correct huge theory, but verification is still logically possible. This second limit for knowledge is thus not an "in-principle" one, so we do not yet have counterexamples here to the verifiability principle—true but interestingly unknowable propositions. Schlick

(1959a,b) noted with some care half a century ago that 'verifiability' must be interpreted in this strong way. And of course at the beginning of the century Peirce had insisted on identifying true propositions with the result of pursuit of inquiry to an *ideal* limit.

Assuming coherence of the concept of such a hypothetical limit, the problem for this, like many other idealizations, is that as we progressively idealize the inquirer, his verification procedures, and his resulting total theory, his God-like omniscience becomes less and less applicable to real cases. The fact that our present cognitive limitations might not be retained in the ideal case, or successive approximations to it, is radically irrelevant to the predicament of the finite human investigator. For example, evolutionary theory does not make it implausible that creatures more intelligent than ourselves may someday slouch over the horizon. But if the Martians or whatever brought us today a perfect oracle or a Doomsday Book containing (one of perhaps many alternative versions of) the final theory, it is likely we could not understand or use much of it. Indeed, how could we even recognize it as an ideal theory? The antirealist's ideal theory seems to serve the epistemological function of the realist's thing-in-itself; if this maneuver yields an improvement in epistemic accessibility, it is only by an epsilon. The idealizers' victory thus is Pyrrhic: the idealizations amount to granting a skeptical conclusion for anything like our situation. It is impossible for *us* to know the whole truth.

Indeed, the argument for these limits for knowledge applies not only to human beings, but to *any* creature of finite resources, even if those constitute the entire known universe. A more extreme idealization of the investigator is agent-as-Turing-machine, with no fixed limit on memory or computing time. It is very important to remember, though, that even such an inquirer, using purely formal procedures, still faces simple but absolutely unsolvable deductive questions, such as the Halting Problem. In this sense, the unattainability of a Peircean ideal limit seems *at least* as severe, and philosophically important, as the unsolvability of the Halting Problem. (An even more idealized investigator might not be restricted, as Turing machines are, to executing algorithms of finite size.) Although philosophy may not be especially interested in limitations imposed by, for instance, everyday carelessness (but recall chapter 5), it is also not solely concerned with highly idealized investigators. We must deal with the intermediate case of the basic epistemological predicament of actual organisms with limited cognitive resources, such as ourselves—this seems the least controversial part of naturalism.

6.6 The Minimal Agent

In fact, the argument of this chapter against perfect epistemic agents can be conceived of as part of the general program of this book, to construct a philosophical theory of a minimal agent that is less idealized than standard decision-theoretic inspired ones. The typical idealization requires the agent to have a perfect capacity to choose actions appropriate for his belief-desire set; that in turn requires the agent to be able to make virtually any deductive inferences from his beliefs. We have seen that, for such an agent, much of the deductive sciences would be trivial. This therefore has seemed a profoundly inapplicable idealization, not just a harmless approximation of actual human rationality.

And the program of developing less idealized theories of the minimally rational epistemic agent for empirical as well as deductive sciences meshes with two extraphilosophical areas discussed in earlier chapters that are the focus of much recent research: psychological studies of prima facie "irrational" human reasoning, and complexity theory in computer science. The "psychology of irrationality" reveals remarkably persistent and ubiquitous use of formally incorrect heuristics in everyday reasoning. Complexity theory indicates quite stringent practical limitations on even ideal computers with literally the resources of the entire universe; we have seen that in some ways it is as if, as a practical matter, Church's Undecidability Theorem applied to formally correct decision procedures all the way down to tautology testing. The "quick and dirty" heuristics may therefore be indispensable to do better than guessing while avoiding computational paralysis. Of course, such imperfect procedures cannot suffice for an ideal agent. Positive skepticism fits in with the above two areas; it thereby gains additional systematicity and explanatory power. For the opposing tendency, to idealize away the "psychological reality" of our cognitive limitations, makes it easy to overlook the important implausibility of the hypothesis that in principle we can know everything.

Indeed, the above picture, suggesting such unexpectedly restricted knowledge of the computational universe, by itself seems to heighten awareness of an appearance/reality distinction. It reinforces the realist view that there are objective computational facts—for instance, primality of some large integer, or truth-functional consistency of a set of propositions—existing independently of our knowledge-gathering activities. Furthermore, the picture of extensive practical uncomputability motivates unfolding the traditional philosophical dichotomy between in-principle logical and "mere" practical impossibility into a trichotomy. Practical impossibility may sometimes involve only current technological unfeasibility, but sometimes it involves principled limitations as hard to evade as computational intractability. If a task must require resources greater than those of the entire universe, that can be philosophically significant, not just an engineering obstacle, even though the task remains "in principle" possible—for instance, for a more ideal investigator that, like a Turing machine, has potentially infinite memory space and computing time.

6.7 A Kantian Argument

The above arguments for limits for knowledge are empirically based, in that they conclude that the hypothesis 'Our theories can be complete and completely correct' at least can be empirically disconfirmed. This approach is worth contrasting briefly with stronger, a priori arguments that we cannot even make sense of this hypothesis. One part of the discussion of the antinomies of the "ideas of reason" in the Dialectic of Kant's *Critique of Pure Reason* (1929, bk. II, chap. 2) contains the most important basis for an argument that we cannot accept the hypothesis that we could know everything. For example, in the conclusion to the later *Prolegomena to Any Future Metaphysics*, Kant asserts,

We cannot . . . , beyond all possible experience, form a definite concept of what things in themselves may be. Yet we are not at liberty to abstain entirely from inquiring into them; for experience never satisfies reason fully but, in answering questions, refers us further and further back and leaves us dissatisfied with regard to their complete solution. (1950, 100)

Skirting intricacies of the larger Kantian program, we can note that on the one hand, Kant's first sentence above expresses the empiricist strain of his account: further, "if even the pure concepts of the understanding are thought to go beyond objects of experience to things in themselves (*noumena*), they have no meaning whatever" (p. 60). This theme is familiar from our earlier critique of verificationism. On the other hand, the second sentence asserts that if unexperienceable things in themselves are nonsense, they are for us *indispensable* nonsense. Again, "It would be, on the other hand, a still greater absurdity if we conceded no things in themselves . . ." (p. 99); such ideas have a necessary regulative role in the conduct of science.

In particular, Kant's argument here seems to imply, among other things, that we cannot make sense of the notion of the completion of scientific inquiry, the end-state in terms of which Peirce defined truth. For instance, we cannot conceive of any end to "why" questions. One such argument might proceed by a kind of inductive schema: (1) Initial case: We require explanations of everyday, observable phenomena. (2) Inductive step: Given any current basic level of general explanation, we can always ask the "child's question" of why in turn that explanatory story holds. We cannot seem to imagine an answer that would terminate this series of questions at any stage of inquiry. For example, one might attempt to stop the "atom-proton-quark . . ." regress by just postulating an infinite hierarchy of sub-quark-like objects; but then one can ask about the causes of this hierarchy itself and its properties. (In the discussion of the cosmological antinomies Kant of course also argued that we cannot imagine the world without a first cause; however, Kant's final view, and its rationale, seem to be as quoted above from the conclusion of the *Prolegomena*.) At least this much of the Kantian account seems to entail that we cannot even find it intelligible that we might not be in this type of Sisyphean predicament.

Thus, part of human nature is to raise empirically intractable questions.[6] And, at least from our perspective, this uncompletability of inquiry seems to hold for any finite epistemic agent, not just human beings. If Descartes's Evil Demon had finite cognitive resources, he would confront the same predicament, of endless questions that must eventually outrun those limited resources. For the deductive sciences, of course, we know that a creature with a finitely represented formal deductive capacity—even with potentially infinite memory and computing time—is limited by the classical undecidability results. (A more idealized intelligence might possess the omniscience studied in rational theology. One question is whether the concept of such supernaturally unlimited capacities is coherent. Also, a finite intelligence that encountered such an apparently perfect being would face a special other Minds problem: could the finite agent have any good reason to conclude that the other being was in fact omniscient, rather than just very smart? Further examination of the various notions of the ideal limit of inquiry would be worthwhile.)

The most important question this glance at Kant has raised is, Could we ever eliminate positive skepticism and know, or even have some justification for thinking, that we had eliminated it? In the most manageable and apparently comprehensible universe our criteria for acceptability of empirical theories will still be seen to be at least partially subjectively based and hence to that extent suspect, and the obviously limited nature of our intellectual capacities will cast doubt on the assumption that we can know everything. Paradoxically, it might be that the universe is in fact comprehensible for creatures of finite intelligence such as ourselves, but even if it were, we would still have some good reason to overshoot, to reject such a cosmology. The belief in our limits may therefore itself be a part of our unavoidable acceptability biases. In this way, a belief in limits for our knowledge seems more than just an accident of the current zeitgeist.

Beginning with basic features of our theory of ourselves as epistemic agents, our picture of our universe, and the relation of one to the other, I have argued against the widespread positivist viewpoint expressed in this passage from Ayer's *Language, Truth, and Logic*:

One way of attacking a metaphysician who claimed to have knowledge of a reality which transcended the phenomenal world would be to inquire from what premises his propositions were deduced. Must he not begin, as other men do, with the evidence of his senses? And if so, what valid process of reasoning can possibly lead him to the conception of a transcendent reality? (1946, 33)

I have suggested that as we try to deny an appearance/reality distinction by means of such verificationist strategies, whether explicit or implicit, the distinction reimposes itself and questions rather like the traditional philosophical ("skeptigenic") ones arise again.

Reducing philosophy to science does not evade them. Thus, epistemology *redivivus*: In this respect, Richard Rorty's announcements of the death of epistemology (for instance, Rorty 1979) seem premature, since science itself, in motivating doubts about the future of progress, still distinguishes between mere correctness of game-playing within its own disciplinary matrix, and truth. Similarly, contrary to Putnam's recent arguments for "internal realism" along something of the lines of Quine's earlier "no cosmic exile" point, an external "metaphysical" realism seems not to require the impossibility of a God's-eye view extratheoretical skyhook; rather, it is a consequence of our world view itself.

Unlike traditional skepticism about, for instance, existence of physical objects, the skepticism here is positively supported, but it is nonspecific—we cannot now say exactly what it is we do not and cannot know. In this way, 'However reality is, it is unlikely to be as we believe it to be' is the ultimate Preface Paradox. Therefore, as with traditional skepticism, we should not worry in practical or scientific matters about this type of skepticism— in particular, withdraw acceptance of all our current theories. Ex hypothesi, these theories are the best we presently have. Similarly, despite this shortcoming of the verifiability principle, the recommendation is of course not that science give up and become fanciful nonempirical speculation, any more than that a basic desideratum like simplicity be abandoned. The bearing of this skepticism is rather within traditional theory of knowledge. It tells us something about ourselves, part of our relation to the world. It indicates types of limits for knowledge that recent philosophy has tended to overlook, because of pervasive overidealization of the epistemic agent.

Notes

Chapter 1

1. In Russell 1971, 311. Vermazen (1968) proposes one of a number of more recent similar views.

2. One of the earliest and most influential discussions was in part IV of Simon 1957.

3. See the discussion of the distinctiveness of this type of causal efficacy in Davidson 1980a,b. (In sections 4.4 and 4.5 I will examine the specific causal role of beliefs in logical laws.)

4. Regresses of a similar type were discussed in Ryle 1949, chap. 2.

5. An experimental study of such preference intransitivities that has achieved something of the status of a classic is Tversky 1969. (Cohen (1981) attacks the intelligibility of the very idea of people's use of formally incorrect inference procedures; for criticism of Cohen's account, see note 18 of chapter 4.) A review of a much earlier and separate line of empirical research on "consistency theory," in the psychology of attitudes and beliefs, can be found in McGuire 1969; see also chapter 3.

6. Appropriateness here again must be evaluated relative to the agent's beliefs, not the objective facts, since it would be an unacceptably extreme idealization to assume the agent's beliefs are always correct. However, we have seen that these beliefs are subject to an "objective" consistency constraint.

7. Simon (1957) is well known in decision theory for having made the similar point that an agent ought to attempt only to "satisfice" rather than to "maximize." (To reply that the standard principle of perfect maximization is now also to be self-applied to choices about how to expend the agent's limited cognitive resources will just again introduce infinite regress.)

Chapter 2

1. This simplified model of inference therefore can be contrasted with, for instance, the account in Harman 1973.

2. For our purposes, two kinds of belief attribution should be distinguished. On the one hand, the assertion 'John believes $p \lor -p$' says that, for a sentence p, John believes the disjunction $p \lor -p$; for example, John might believe the English sentence 'It's raining or it isn't raining'. On the other hand, the

assertion 'John believes '$p \lor -p$'' says that John believes or accepts the logical law of the excluded middle, and not just instances of the law.

3. Hintikka seems to have supposed, to the contrary, that there is some objective measure of the difficulty of an inference that must apply to all reasoners. Hintikka says, "If this consequence-relation [of p to what I know] is a distant one, I may fail to know, in a perfectly good sense, that p is the case, for I may fail to see that p follows from what I know" (1962, 30; see also p. 35). The suggestion seems to be that the "remoteness" of the logical relation between two statements is independent of, for instance, the deductive system used by the reasoner. See also Hintikka 1970, especially p. 147.

4. This axiom corresponds to one of the basic inference rules of, among others, the deductive system of Kleene (1967, 107).

5. See Prior's (1967) earlier attack upon and Belnap's (1967) defense of the thesis that the connectives can be defined in terms of the role they play in deductions—ones that this chapter would classify as "obvious."

6. See the important qualifications of Quine's assertion in Putnam 1975/6, sec. 3. The point seems to remain that accepting certain logical laws is necessary, even if not sufficient, for the identity of a constant.

7. The sentences expressing the two putative beliefs are of the form '$(\exists x) (\forall y) (Fx \rightarrow Gy)$' and '$(\forall x)Fx \rightarrow (\forall x)Gx$', respectively.

8. Of course, the presuppositions of this claim conflict with Davidson's (1984b) "no language, no thought" position. The claim is also contrary to Bennett's assertion, "We cannot have grounds for crediting a languageless creature with moderate logical acumen" (1976, 116); in the terminology used here, only a null or universal feasibility ordering supposedly can apply to such a creature. Briefly, Bennett's conclusion for the type of example we are now considering seems to be based on, among other things, taking for granted (pp. 116–117) that the feasibility ordering for a "normal" human's verbal beliefs will be the ordering for the verbal beliefs of any creature.

Chapter 3

1. There is a second way of interpreting Quine's assertion about the revisability relations among beliefs. Such a "normative" interpretation corresponds to that usually adopted for axiomatizations of decision theory and epistemic logic: the entailment between changing one belief and changing a logically related one may not be recognized and acted upon at all by the agent. According to this interpretation, if the agent is to be "rational" at least in some narrowly epistemic sense, and in particular if he is to maintain perfect consistency, he must (or ought), after rejecting the one belief, to reject the other. Since Quine's assertion then does not involve any prediction that the agent will in fact make the appropriate reevaluation, this interpretation seems to be excluded in favor of the descriptive interpretation of the passages cited in the text. However, many discussions of rationality, including sometimes Quine's (for instance, in the last section of 1961a), do not always distinguish between normative and descriptive rationality theses. To the extent that they do not, strong idealizations of the agent that might be appropriate as part of a norma-

tive account then acquire unwarranted plausibility as part of a descriptive account, as noted in section 1.8.

2. A typical text is Howe 1970; Klatzky 1975 surveys several recent approaches in psychology of memory. An alternative to, or elaboration of, the traditional duplex theory is a "levels of processing" theory (see Craik and Lockhart 1972). The nature of the difference between the two accounts needs clarification; the levels of processing theory still seems to include the main element of the duplex theory, a distinction between activated and inactive items.

3. As a classic example, see Collins and Quillian 1969; a text of this school is Lindsay and Norman 1977, chaps. 8–10.

4. The *locus classicus* is Bartlett 1932; a more recent influential discussion was Neisser 1967, especially chaps. 8 and 11. See also Bransford and Franks 1971.

5. For Quine's view, see 1960, chap. 2, especially p. 59. Davidson's preference transitivity requirement was reviewed in chapter 1. (Descartes, however, was aware of intransitivity phenomena. See rule VII of his *Rules for the Direction of the Mind* (1955a).) On the *modus ponens* inference, see, for example, Black 1970, 21; using in effect a portion of the commonsense duplex model, de Sousa rejects similar positions (1971, especially pp. 65, 73).

6. On the basic design of efficient data structures, see Knuth 1973; for a review of search methods in artificial intelligence, see Winston 1977, chap. 4.

Chapter 4

1. See, respectively, Quine 1960, 58, and Quine 1970, 102. Some of Quine's discussion of translation can be construed as entailing only universal *nonrejectability* of logic. See section 4.10 for an argument that correct translation might attribute rejection of any particular logical truths.

2. Two key papers on computational complexity are Cook 1971 and Karp 1972. Garey and Johnson 1979 reviews part of the field: NP-completeness. Two easily accessible articles are Lewis and Papadimitriou 1978 and Stockmeyer and Chandra 1979. Cook 1983 is a recent historical survey of the field.

3. See the discussion of the concept of a decision procedure in Kleene 1967, sec. 40, for examples of the relegation of such "practical" issues to the applied sciences.

4. The traveling salesman problem, an NP-complete network-design problem of considerable practical interest in operations research, is this: given a set of cities on a map and all intercity distances, construct the optimum tour, that is, the shortest round-trip route connecting all cities. As of the early 1980s the largest unconstrained set of points for which a proved exact traveling salesman tour had been found contained only 318 points. (See Kirkpatrick, Gelatt, and Vecchi 1983, 679. This paper introduces "statistical mechanics algorithms" for approximate optimization solutions that differ quite interestingly from conventional discrete-mathematics techniques.) For purposes of comparison, there are more than 318 towns in the state of Tennessee.

5. For a review of some of their own basic work by two major contributors to the field, see Tversky and Kahneman 1974; a recent overview is Nisbett and Ross 1980.

6. Recall also the argument in section 2.5 against the claim that being able to make particular "obvious" inferences, by whatever means, is *constitutive* of understanding the logical constants involved in those inferences; the argument would apply in particular against the assertion that strong acceptance— that is, actual use—of the corresponding obvious valid laws or sound rules is required for an agent to qualify as understanding the logical constants involved.

7. The question of adopting convenient but in some sense unsound inference rules in fact sometimes is raised in devising natural deduction systems for introductory logic texts; see, for example, Mates 1972, vii.

8. An early (and controversial) study suggesting that subjects use a kind of global impression or "atmosphere" of the logical form of an inference was Woodworth and Sells 1935; see also Wason and Johnson-Laird 1972, chap. 10. For a review of research on prototypicality, see Rosch 1977.

On the use of a prototypicality heuristic in deductive inference, see Cherniak 1984. Briefly, the heuristic is this: To determine validity of a proof, (1) only test the proof for specific examples of the categories involved, and (2) pick typical or "good" rather than arbitrary examples (for instance, for the "bird" category, "robin" rather than "turkey"). The arguments studied were of the simplest sort, for instance, 'Some A's are birds. / Some A's are robins'. The basic prediction was that if people used this heuristic, their performance (for instance, error rates) should show a strong interaction between whether or not the inference was valid and whether or not the example involved was prototypical: prototypicality should help performance on valid inferences but hinder invalid ones.

At least on these "toy" logic problems, the subjects seemed able to choose whether or not to use the heuristic. If the time available for each problem was "clamped"—even at double the time earlier subjects took when time was not fixed—subjects' performance showed the predicted interaction for use of the heuristic. In addition, subjects' "metaheuristic" decision to shift to the heuristic over the course of a series of logic problems seemed to be advisable, in that error rates then dropped. The logic problems were drawn from the monadic predicate calculus, for which decision algorithms are known to be computationally complex (see Lewis 1978); subjects' use of a quick but dirty heuristic here is thus consistent with the working hypothesis of a real-world antagonism between formal correctness and tractability.

9. See Rabin 1974. On Rabin's concept of a probabilistic algorithm, see Rabin 1976. Rabin's argument is reported in Kolata 1976.

10. Putnam (1975a) has also argued, in a Quinian vein, that "quasi-empirical" methods—resembling those employed in evaluating the plausibility, for instance, of highly theoretical statements in physics—have always been important in mathematics outside the domain of formal proof.

11. For an earlier investigation of probability-distribution, as opposed to worst-case, analyses, see Karp 1976. A recent bibliography of this area, with some commentary, is Karp et al. 1985.

12. For the proof that the simplex algorithm requires exponential time, see Klee and Minty 1972. The "empirical" study of running times is in McCall 1982. Smale's proof can be found in Smale 1983; it was also reported in *Science* 217 (1982), 39. Lovacs 1980 briefly reviews the so-called Khachian algorithm.

13. With the speed of light 299,726 km/sec and a nucleon 10^{-13} cm in diameter (see, for example, Knuth 1976), the "supercycle" time would be around 2.9×10^{-23} sec. Thus, the maximum number of cycles available would be 2.9×10^{23} cycles $\times$ 60 sec $\times$ 60 min $\times$ 24 hrs $\times$ 365 days $\times$ 2×10^{10} years, which is less than 2×10^{41} cycles. But the truth table contains 2^{138} lines, which is more than 3×10^{41} lines; hence, checking one line per supercycle, the machine could not evaluate this truth table during the entire history of the universe.

14. Undecidability for elementary arithmetic is now known not to arise only for extremely complex and mathematically uninteresting sentences. See Jones 1978 for an undecidable, unabbreviated sentence (based on the solution of Hilbert's Tenth Problem) of about 100 symbols in length, and Jones 1982 for the basis for constructing still shorter sentences. (See also Chaitin 1974.) In addition, a "mathematically simple and interesting" theorem (an extension of the finite Ramsey Theorem) is not provable in Peano arithmetic; see Paris and Harrington 1977. The discussion in this chapter further motivates study of the "density," or distribution, of absolutely undecidable sentences.

15. For example, as noted, the set of theorems of Presburger arithmetic has early-onset complexity. However, the set of Presburger arithmetic theorems, each of length more than 10,000 symbols, can be quickly decided for any case of length fewer than 10,000 symbols; the algorithm will just count the number of symbols in any sentence to be decided and immediately reject it if there are fewer than 10,000. Another question concerns the "naturalness" of such truncated problems.

16. Correspondingly, in artificial intelligence the algorithmic approach of seeking classical decision procedures, or even just complete proof procedures, for theoremhood needs to be reevaluated in light of the problem of combinatorial explosion of branchings in proofs. For a brief discussion of the issue, see Newell and Simon 1976; see also Rabin 1974. An extensive review of practical limitations on theorem-proving programs (and program verifiers) still is needed.

17. Berwick and Weinberg 1984, chaps. 3 and 4, contains one of the first sustained discussions of implications of computational complexity theory for an area of cognitive science. Berwick and Weinberg argue that complexity-theoretic constraints are not relevant to models of natural language parsers. The first reason given is the "relevant range problem": the typical sentence length that the human parsing mechanism confronts is only about 10 words, but "worst-case" complexity measures cannot be shown to apply in a significant way for such a size range. In reply, however, it should be noted that the problem of making inferences from a human belief set involves an entirely different regime of input size. A person's total belief set (and important subsets) can be of virtually unbounded size; an inference-engine, in contrast

to a parser, therefore confronts a much more "relevant range" of input size (recall the combinatorial explosion for consistency-testing a belief set with only 138 independent propositions). Prospects for staving off complexity constraints seem less favorable when a problem cannot be restricted to only sentence-by-sentence processing. In addition, as discussed earlier, there are some cases of known early-onset complexity, such as WS1S and Presburger arithmetic.

In arguing for the real-world irrelevance of complexity theory, Berwick and Weinberg also cite the "implementation problem": complexity estimates for an algorithm depend on its implementation—the nature of the representational format and processing operations—but these are presently unknown for the human brain. However, it seems worth keeping in mind that most workers in the very real-world fields of operations research would agree that perfect algorithms for the satisfiability or traveling salesman problems are just plain costly for any plausible implementations of these algorithms.

Berwick and Weinberg point out that mathematically interesting properties (like asymptotic computational complexity) tend not to fit well with real-world properties (such as inefficient parsability). But this seems a virtually inevitable feature of applying formal models to empirical reality, whether the formally manageable concept is that of an ideal gas or of Turing-computability. As we have seen, such imperfect matching does not in itself make the formalization strategy valueless. The approach of this chapter has been not to demand verification in advance that there is real-world relevant computational complexity, but instead to treat the claim that there is such complexity as a working hypothesis, and then to see what varieties of "data" (broadly construed) can be interestingly explained within such a framework.

18. A very natural proposal is that the logical ability of an agent should be thought of as a "logical competence" on the model of linguistic competence. (See, for example, Cohen 1981). The fundamental datum of departures of actual human reasoning from ideal models is then treated as a performance deficit, like the deficits apparent for the linguistic competence of an ideal speaker-hearer as a result of time and memory limitations, and so forth. There are then two alternative hypotheses—perhaps, pessimistically, two Kuhnian paradigms—to account for actual suboptimal deductive performance. According to a minimal rationality account, human beings might just be using a metatheoretically inadequate deductive system involving fast but fallacious heuristics that are generally practically adequate. According to the ideal competence account, humans have a perfect underlying deductive competence in the form of acceptance of a metatheoretically adequate deductive system; observed reasoning errors arise because the logic is applied improperly, as a result of the performance obstructions.

However, the notion of a logical competence does not seem especially helpful here because of types of problems already evident in *Meno* for Socrates' attribution to the servant of knowledge of the Pythagorean Theorem: if the servant really believed the theorem before Socrates talked to him, why couldn't he *use* it then? Although any hypothesis can be held true come what may, the perfect competence account seems to gain epicycles too fast. Eventually, it amounts to saying that an agent accepts a metatheoretically adequate logic; he just usually misapplies it because, for example, in Cohen's words, eliciting conditions are "rarely, if ever, ideal for the exercise of such a competence" (1981, 322). Rather than attempting a principled account, a classical competence/performance distinction must explain away a wide range of actual behavior as "mere" exceptions, as insignificant "noise."

In addition, why must the competence be in the form of a metatheoretically, rather than practically, adequate system? A system that is perspicuous from the standpoint of linguist or logical theorist may not be efficiently processable by the agent. As we have seen, a system that is adequate from the former standpoint may not be processable at all; the antagonism between formal correctness and tractability makes the ideal competence account seem particularly unrealistic. Indeed, the notion of accepting a logic involved in the notion of abstract competence seems in some danger of equivocation between our strong and weak senses of "acceptance." Is the ideal speaker-hearer (or an actual human being) *really* supposed to use the perfect logic, or not? A psychologically realistic concept of "minimal competence" seems to have some advantages.

Chapter 5

1. On contemporary law of torts, see Holmes 1963, chap. 2, and Prosser 1971. For discussion of some of the relevant philosophy of law, see Hart and Honoré 1959, chap. 6. On the historical development of the legal concept of negligence, see Baker 1979, chap. 17; for a review of negligence and the reasonable man doctrine, particularly in the medieval era, see Winfield 1926.

Of course, tort law is not an idiosyncrasy of English and American common law. On the comparable "law of obligations" in the present Napoleonic code, see Weill 1971. The notion in ancient Roman law of *diligens pater familias* ("the good housekeeper") seems closely related to our reasonable man concept; Greuber (1886, especially pp. 222–233) describes it. Similar ideas can be found in ancient Assyrian and Talmudic codes. For some cross-cultural studies of legal reasonable man concepts in contemporary pretechnological societies, see Gluckman 1967, chap. 3, and Pospisil 1971, for example, pp. 240–245. (It would be interesting to examine legal concepts in China before contact with the West.)

The fact that a reasonable person concept turns up in such disparate social structures further suggests its universality. A cross-cultural hypothesis worth some systematic exploration, therefore, is that the reasonable person concept is as universal as the very idea of a legal code.

2. Austin's inference from a knowledge claim's not being subject to criticism even when it turns out to be wrong, to the conclusion that in this case the utterer of the claim actually *did* have knowledge, seems weak. (See Austin 1979, especially pp. 97–103.) Rather, it just seems inappropriate, on Gricean grounds of irrelevance sketched above, to attack the utterer then by pointing out, 'So you *didn't* know'. On Austin's failure in this way to distinguish semantics from pragmatics, see Stroud 1984, chap. 2. Stroud also argues against the idea that a special reasons requirement eliminates skepticism, as has Cavell (1979).

3. Quotation from "The Fixation of Belief." See also "Critical Commonsensism" and "The Scientific Attitude and Fallibilism," in Peirce 1932.

4. See Dennett's (1978a) (rather instrumentalistic) discussion of "belief-analogues" in chess-playing machines.

5. A rather successful short compendium of this title was edited by Duncan and Weston-Smith (1977).

6. Such preliminary tentative assumptions about typical or normal cases resemble automatic "default settings" in knowledge structures in artificial intelligence; see Minsky 1975. In Gestalt terms, unexamined possibilities may be conceived of as the "ground" against which we consider the "figure" of a limited set of possibly relevant cases; for a Gestalt account of problem solving, see Duncker 1968.

In addition, if assumptions are treated as a type of tool, the idea of an assumption being taken for granted can perhaps be illuminated a little by Heidegger's discussion in *Being and Time* (1962, especially chap. 4) of people's unawareness of the implements they use. When we employ familiar equipment, it tends to be "ready to hand," to disappear from our consciousness; our attention shifts to the tool—it becomes conspicuous or "present to hand"—when its normal usability is disturbed.

Chapter 6

1. Lewis (1984) reaches a similarly embarrassing conclusion, by quite different arguments, for Putnam's (1978) reference-theoretic argument that an ideally verified theory cannot be false.

2. See also "On the Very Idea of a Third Dogma" (especially p. 41), in Quine 1981. Quine seems to agree in spirit with a remark Neurath endorsed in "Protokolsätze" on almost the same page as the boat analogy: "One ought to be able to make the outlines of any rigorously scientific thesis comprehensible in his own terms to a hackney-coach-driver" (1959, 200). See also the similar remark cited by Hilbert (1935).

3. Davidson 1984a, 198. An argument that resembles Davidson's in some respects appeared earlier in Stroud 1969, especially pp. 90–94.

4. On charity, see Davidson 1984b, 169 (also p. 159). (Davidson also sometimes endorses apparently moderate charity principles (for instance, elsewhere in the above paper); he does not seem to distinguish moderate from extreme charity.) On preference transitivity, see Davidson 1980b, 237.

5. Fodor (1975) has arrived by very different means at a "no news" conclusion rather like Davidson's: "There can be no such thing as learning a new concept" (p. 95). Fodor's argument is based on the innateness hypothesis that all human beings employ the same species-specific internal "language of thought," into which any public natural-language expression must be translatable in order to be understood. (Martians with conceptual schemes differing from that of *Homo sapiens* are therefore not necessarily impossible, just inevitably unintelligible to us. The Martians would correspondingly be locked into their own innate conceptual inventory.) Like Davidson, Fodor assumes that understanding can occur only by means of direct translation. Some of the paradoxicality of Fodor's conclusion dissipates if one distinguishes between acquiring new elementary concepts and acquiring new complex ones; at most, the argument seems to apply to the former. (Given this semantic ultranativ-

ism, it is not surprising that more recently Fodor has broached, if not ventured to answer, the question of whether the mind is "epistemically bounded," that is, constrained in its knowledge by its cognitive organization; see Fodor 1983, 119–126.)

6. Compare Hume's earlier remark, ". . . 'tis almost impossible for the mind of man to rest, like those of beasts, in that narrow circle of objects, which are the subject of daily conversation and action" (1965, 271). The very first sentence of the *Critique of Pure Reason* (1929, 7) already goes beyond Hume here.

References

Austin, J. (1979). *Philosophical Papers*, 3rd ed., J. Urmson and G. Warnock, eds. New York: Oxford University Press.

Ayer, A. (1946). *Language, Truth, and Logic*. London: Gollancz.

Ayer, A., ed. (1959). *Logical Positivism*. New York: Free Press.

Baker, J. (1979). *Introduction to English Legal History*, 2nd ed. London: Butterworths.

Bar-Hillel, Y. (1964). "Is Information-Retrieval Approaching a Crisis?" In *Language and Information*. Reading, Mass.: Addison-Wesley.

Bartlett, F. (1932). *Remembering: A Study in Experimental and Social Psychology*. Cambridge: Cambridge University Press.

Belnap, N. (1967). "Tonk, Plonk, and Plink." In *Philosophical Logic*, P. Strawson, ed. Oxford: Oxford University Press.

Bennett, J. (1976). *Linguistic Behavior*. New York: Cambridge University Press.

Bergson, H. (1911). *Creative Evolution*. New York: Henry Holt.

Berwick, R., and A. Weinberg (1984). *The Grammatical Basis of Linguistic Performance*. Cambridge, Mass.: The MIT Press.

Black, M. (1970). "The Justification of Logical Axioms." In *The Margins of Precision*. Ithaca, N.Y.: Cornell University Press.

Bransford, J., and J. Franks (1971). "The Abstraction of Linguistic Ideas." *Cognitive Psychology* 2, 331–350.

Campbell, D. (1974). "Evolutionary Epistemology." In *The Philosophy of Karl Popper*, P. Schilpp, ed. La Salle, Ill.: Open Court.

Carnap, R. (1956). "Empiricism, Semantics, and Ontology." In *Meaning and Necessity*, 2nd ed. Chicago: University of Chicago Press.

Cavell, S. (1979). *The Claim of Reason*. New York: Oxford University Press.

Chaitin, G. (1974). "Information-Theoretic Limitations of Formal Systems." *Journal of the Association for Computing Machinery* 21, 403–424.

Cherniak, C. (1984). "Prototypicality and Deductive Reasoning." *Journal of Verbal Learning and Verbal Behavior* 23, 625–642.

Church, A. (1956). *Introduction to Mathematical Logic*, vol. 1. Princeton, N.J.: Princeton University Press.

Cohen, L. (1981). "Can Human Irrationality Be Experimentally Demonstrated?" *Behavioral and Brain Sciences* 4, 317–331.

Collins, A., and M. Quillian (1969). "Retrieval Time from Semantic Memory." *Journal of Verbal Learning and Verbal Behavior* 8, 240–247.

Cook, S. (1971). "The Complexity of Theorem-Proving Procedures." *Proceedings of the 3rd Annual ACM Symposium on Theory of Computing*, 151–158.

Cook, S. (1983). "An Overview of Computational Complexity." *Communications of the Association for Computing Machinery* 26, 400–408.

Cornsweet, T. (1970). *Visual Perception.* New York: Academic Press.

Craik, F., and R. Lockhart (1972). "Levels of Processing: A Framework for Memory Research." *Journal of Verbal Learning and Verbal Behavior* 11, 671–684.

Davidson, D. (1980a). "Actions, Reasons, and Causes." In Davidson (1980d).

Davidson, D. (1980b). "Psychology as Philosophy." In Davidson (1980d).

Davidson, D. (1980c). "Mental Events." In Davidson (1980d).

Davidson, D. (1980d). *Essays on Actions and Events.* New York: Oxford University Press.

Davidson, D. (1984a). "On the Very Idea of a Conceptual Scheme." In Davidson (1984c).

Davidson, D. (1984b). "Thought and Talk." In Davidson (1984c).

Davidson, D. (1984c). *Inquiries into Truth and Interpretation.* New York: Oxford University Press.

Davidson, D., and J. Hintikka, eds. (1969). *Words and Objections.* Dordrecht: D. Reidel.

Dennett, D. (1978a). "Intentional Systems." In Dennett (1978c).

Dennett, D. (1978b). "Conditions of Personhood." In Dennett (1978c).

Dennett, D. (1978c). *Brainstorms.* Cambridge, Mass.: The MIT Press. A Bradford book.

Descartes, R. (1955a). *Rules for the Direction of the Mind.* In Descartes (1955d).

Descartes, R. (1955b). *Meditations.* In Descartes (1955d).

Descartes, R. (1955c). *The Principles of Philosophy.* In Descartes (1955d).

Descartes, R. (1955d). *Philosophical Works,* vol. 1, E. Haldane and G. Ross, tr. Cambridge: Cambridge University Press.

de Sousa, R. (1971). "How to Give a Piece of Your Mind; or the Logic of Belief and Assent." *Review of Metaphysics* 25, 52–79.

de Sousa, R. (1976). "Rational Homunculi." In *The Identity of Persons,* A. Rorty, ed. Berkeley, Calif.: University of California Press.

Dretske, F. (1981). *Knowledge and the Flow of Information.* Cambridge, Mass.: The MIT Press. A Bradford book.

Du Bois-Reymond, E. (1872). *Über die Grenzen des Naturerkennens.* Leipzig: Veit.

Dummett, M. (1978). *Truth and Other Enigmas*. Cambridge, Mass.: Harvard University Press.

Duncan, R., and M. Weston-Smith, eds. (1977). *Encyclopedia of Ignorance*. New York: Simon and Schuster.

Duncker, K. (1968). "On Problem-Solving." In Wason and Johnson-Laird, eds. (1968).

Fischer, M., and M. Rabin (1974). "Super-Exponential Complexity of Presburger Arithmetic." *Complexity of Computation, SIAM-AMS Proceedings* 7, 27–41.

Fodor, J. (1975). *The Language of Thought*. New York: Crowell.

Fodor, J. (1983). *The Modularity of Mind*. Cambridge, Mass.: The MIT Press. A Bradford book.

Garey, M., and D. Johnson (1979). *Computers and Intractability*. San Francisco: W. H. Freeman.

Gluckman, M. (1967). *The Judicial Process among the Barotse of Northern Rhodesia*, 2nd ed. New York: Humanities Press.

Goldman, A. (1976). "Discrimination and Perceptual Knowledge." *Journal of Philosophy* 73, 771–791.

Goldman, A. (1978). "Epistemics: The Regulative Theory of Cognition." *Journal of Philosophy* 75, 509–523.

Green, D. (1976). *An Introduction to Hearing*. Hillsdale, N.J.: Lawrence Erlbaum.

Greuber, E. (1886). *The Roman Law of Damage to Property*. Oxford: Clarendon Press.

Grice, H. (1975). "Logic and Conversation." In *The Logic of Grammar*, D. Davidson and G. Harman, eds. Encino, Calif.: Dickenson.

Harman, G. (1973). *Thought*. Princeton, N.J.: Princeton University Press.

Hart, H., and H. Honoré (1959). *Causation in the Law*. Oxford: Oxford University Press.

Heidegger, M. (1962). *Being and Time*. New York: Harper and Row.

Hempel, C. (1965). "Aspects of Scientific Explanation." In *Aspects of Scientific Explanation*. New York: Free Press.

Hilbert, D. (1935). "Mathematische Probleme." In *Gesammelte Abhandlungen*, vol. 3. Berlin: Springer.

Hilding, A. (1975). Letter. *Science* 187, 703.

Hintikka, J. (1962). *Knowledge and Belief*. Ithaca, N.Y.: Cornell University Press.

Hintikka, J. (1970). "Information, Deduction, and the A Priori." *Nous* 4, 135–152.

Holmes, O. (1963). *The Common Law*. Cambridge, Mass.: Harvard University Press.

Howe, M. (1970). *Introduction to Human Memory*. New York: Harper and Row.

Hume, D. (1965). *Treatise of Human Nature*, H. Selby-Bigge, ed. Oxford: Oxford University Press.

Jones, J. (1978). "Three Universal Representations of Recursively Enumerable Sets." *Journal of Symbolic Logic* 43, 335–351.

Jones, J. (1982). "Universal Diophantine Equation." *Journal of Symbolic Logic* 47, 549–571.

Joshi, A. (1982). "Mutual Beliefs in Question-Answer Systems." In *Mutual Knowledge*, N. Smith, ed. New York: Academic Press.

Kant, I. (1929). *Critique of Pure Reason*, N. Kemp Smith, tr. London: Macmillan.

Kant, I. (1950). *Prolegomena to Any Future Metaphysics*, L. Beck, tr. New York: Bobbs-Merrill.

Kant, I. (1959). *Foundations of the Metaphysics of Morals*, L. Beck, tr. New York: Bobbs-Merrill.

Karp, R. (1972). "Reducibility among Combinatorial Problems." In *Complexity of Computer Computations*, R. Miller and J. Thatcher, eds. New York: Plenum Press.

Karp, R. (1976). "Probabilistic Analysis of Some Combinatorial Search Algorithms." In Traub, ed. (1976).

Karp, R., J. Lenstra, C. McDiarmid, and A. Rinnooy Kan (1985). "Probabilistic Analysis." In *Combinatorial Optimization: Annotated Bibliographies*, M. O'hEigeartaigh, J. Lenstra, and A. Rinnooy Kan, eds. New York: John Wiley.

Kirkpatrick, S., C. Gelatt, and M. Vecchi (1983). "Optimization by Simulated Annealing." *Science* 220, 671–680.

Klatzky, R. (1975). *Human Memory: Structures and Processes*. San Francisco: W. H. Freeman.

Klee, V., and G. Minty (1972). "How Good Is the Simplex Algorithm?" In *Inequalities-III*, O. Shisha, ed. New York: Academic Press.

Kleene, S. (1967). *Mathematical Logic*. New York: John Wiley.

Knuth, D. (1973). *The Art of Computer Programming*, vol. 3. Reading, Mass.: Addison-Wesley.

Knuth, D. (1976). "Mathematics and Computer Science: Coping with Finiteness." *Science* 194, 1235–1242.

Kolata, G. (1976). "Mathematical Proofs: The Genesis of Reasonable Doubt." *Science* 192, 989–990.

Kuhn, T. (1970). *The Structure of Scientific Revolutions*, 2nd ed. Chicago: University of Chicago Press.

Lehrer, K. (1974). *Knowledge*. Oxford: Oxford University Press.

Lewis, D. (1984). "Putnam's Paradox." *Australasian Journal of Philosophy* 62, 221–236.

Lewis, H. (1978). "Complexity of Solvable Cases of the Decision Problem for the Predicate Calculus." *Proceedings of the 19th IEEE Symposium on Foundations of Computer Science*, 35–47.

Lewis, H., and C. Papadimitriou (1978). "The Efficiency of Algorithms." *Scientific American* 238, 96–109.

Lindsay, P., and D. Norman (1977). *Human Information Processing.* New York: Academic Press.

Lovacs, L. (1980). "A New Linear Programming Algorithm—Better or Worse than the Simplex Method?" *Mathematical Intelligencer* 2, 141–146.

McCall, E. (1982). "Performance Results of the Simplex Algorithm for a Set of Real-World Linear Programming Models." *Communications of the Association for Computing Machinery* 25, 207–212.

McGuire, W. (1960). "A Syllogistic Analysis of Cognitive Relationships." In *Attitude Organization and Change,* C. Hovland and M. Rosenberg, eds. New Haven, Conn.: Yale University Press.

McGuire, W. (1969). "The Nature of Attitudes and Attitude Change." In *Handbook of Social Psychology,* 2nd ed., G. Lindzey and E. Aronson, eds. Reading, Mass.: Addison-Wesley.

Mates, B. (1972). *Elementary Logic.* New York: Oxford University Press.

Meyer, A. (1975). "Weak Monadic Second-Order Theory of Successor Is Not Elementary-Recursive." In *Lecture Notes in Mathematics,* no. 453, A. Dold and B. Eckmann, eds. New York: Springer-Verlag.

Miller, G. (1956). "The Magical Number Seven Plus or Minus Two: Some Limits of Our Capacity for Processing Information." *Psychological Review* 63, 81–97.

Minsky, M. (1975). "A Framework for Representing Knowledge." In *The Psychology of Computer Vision,* P. Winston, ed. New York: McGraw-Hill.

Morrison, P., and P. Morrison (1981). *Powers of Ten.* San Francisco: W. H. Freeman.

Neisser, U. (1967). *Cognitive Psychology.* Englewood Cliffs, N.J.: Prentice-Hall.

Neurath, O. (1959). "Protocol Sentences." In Ayer, ed. (1959).

Newell, A., and H. Simon (1976). "Computer Science as Empirical Inquiry." *Communications of the Association for Computing Machinery* 19, 113–126.

Nisbett, R., and L. Ross (1980). *Human Inference.* Englewood Cliffs, N.J.: Prentice-Hall.

Paris, J., and L. Harrington (1977). "A Mathematical Incompleteness in Peano Arithmetic." In *Handbook of Mathematical Logic,* J. Barwise, ed. New York: North Holland.

Peirce, C. (1932). *Collected Papers.* Cambridge, Mass.: Harvard University Press.

Plato (1937). *Meno.* In *The Dialogues of Plato,* 3rd ed., B. Jowett, tr. Oxford: Clarendon Press.

Pospisil, L. (1971). *Anthropology of Law: A Comparative Theory.* New York: Harper and Row.

Price, D. (1961). *Science Since Babylon.* New Haven, Conn.: Yale University Press.

Prior, A. (1967). "The Runabout Inference Ticket." In *Philosophical Logic*, P. Strawson, ed. Oxford: Oxford University Press.

Prosser, W. (1971). *Handbook of the Law of Torts*, 4th ed. St. Paul, Minn.: West Publishing Co.

Putnam, H. (1975a). "What Is Mathematical Truth?" In *Philosophical Papers*, vol. 1. New York: Cambridge University Press.

Putnam, H. (1975b). "The Meaning of 'Meaning'." In *Philosophical Papers*, vol. 2. New York: Cambridge University Press.

Putnam, H. (1975/6). "What is 'Realism'?" *Proceedings of the Aristotelian Society* 76, 177–194.

Putnam, H. (1978). "Realism and Reason." In *Meaning and the Moral Sciences*. London: Routledge and Kegan Paul.

Putnam, H. (1981). *Reason, Truth, and History*. Cambridge: Cambridge University Press.

Quine, W. (1960). *Word and Object*. Cambridge, Mass.: The MIT Press.

Quine, W. (1961a). "Two Dogmas of Empiricism." In Quine (1961c).

Quine, W. (1961b). "Identity, Ostension, and Hypostasis." In Quine (1961c).

Quine, W. (1961c). *From a Logical Point of View*. Cambridge, Mass.: Harvard University Press.

Quine, W. (1969a). "Epistemology Naturalized." In Quine (1969d).

Quine, W. (1969b). "Natural Kinds." In Quine (1969d).

Quine, W. (1969c). "Speaking of Objects." In Quine (1969d).

Quine, W. (1969d). *Ontological Relativity*. New York: Columbia University Press.

Quine, W. (1969e). "Reply to Stroud." In Davidson and Hintikka, eds. (1969).

Quine, W. (1970). *Philosophy of Logic*. Englewood Cliffs, N.J.: Prentice-Hall.

Quine, W. (1981). *Theories and Things*. Cambridge, Mass.: Harvard University Press.

Rabin, M. (1974). "Theoretical Impediments to Artificial Intelligence." In *Information Processing 74*, J. Rosenfeld, ed. Amsterdam: North Holland.

Rabin, M. (1976). "Probabilistic Algorithms." In Traub, ed. (1976).

Rorty, R. (1979). *Philosophy and the Mirror of Nature*. Princeton, N.J.: Princeton University Press.

Rosch, E. (1977). "Human Categorization." In *Studies in Cross-Cultural Psychology*, vol. 1, N. Warren, ed. New York: Academic Press.

Russell, B. (1971). *Logic and Knowledge*, R. Marsh, ed. New York: Putnam.

Ryle, G. (1949). *The Concept of Mind*. New York: Barnes and Noble.

Schlick, M. (1959a). "Positivism and Realism." In Ayer, ed. (1959).

Schlick, M. (1959b). "Meaning and Verification." In Ayer, ed. (1959).

Simon, H. (1947). *Administrative Behavior*. New York: Macmillan.

Simon, H. (1957). *Models of Man*. New York: John Wiley.

Smale, S. (1983). "On the Average Number of Steps of the Simplex Method of Linear Programming." *Mathematical Programming* 27, 241–262.

Stockmeyer, L., and A. Chandra (1979). "Intrinsically Difficult Problems." *Scientific American* 240, 140–159.

Stroud, B. (1969). "Conventionalism and the Indeterminacy of Translation." In Davidson and Hintikka, eds. (1969).

Stroud, B. (1979). "Inference, Belief, and Understanding." *Mind* 88, 179–196.

Stroud, B. (1984). *The Significance of Philosophical Skepticism.* Oxford: Oxford University Press.

Tarski, A. (1969). "Truth and Proof." *Scientific American* 220, 63–77.

Traub, J., ed. (1976). *Algorithms and Complexity.* New York: Academic Press.

Tversky, A. (1969). "Intransitivity of Preferences." *Psychological Review* 76, 31–48.

Tversky, A., and D. Kahneman (1974). "Judgment under Uncertainty: Heuristics and Biases." *Science* 185, 1124–1131.

Vermazen, B. (1968). "Consistency and Underdetermination." *Philosophy and Phenomenological Research* 28, 403–409.

Von Neumann, J., and O. Morgenstern (1944). *Theory of Games and Economic Behavior.* Princeton, N.J.: Princeton University Press.

Wason, P., and P. Johnson-Laird, eds. (1968). *Thinking and Reasoning.* London: Penguin.

Wason, P., and P. Johnson-Laird (1972). *Psychology of Reasoning.* Cambridge, Mass.: Harvard University Press.

Weill, A. (1971). *Droit Civil: Les Obligations.* Paris: Dalloz.

Wickelgren, W. (1968). "Sparing of Short-Term Memory in an Amnesiac Patient." *Neuropsychologia* 6, 235–244.

Winfield, P. (1926). "The History of Negligence in the Law of Torts." *Law Quarterly Review* 42, 184–199.

Winston, P. (1977). *Artificial Intelligence.* Reading, Mass.: Addison-Wesley.

Wittgenstein, L. (1976). *Wittgenstein's Lectures on the Foundations of Mathematics: Cambridge, 1939,* C. Diamond, ed. Ithaca, N.Y.: Cornell University Press.

Woodworth, R., and S. Sells (1935). "An Atmosphere Effect in Formal Syllogistic Reasoning." *Journal of Experimental Psychology* 18, 451–460.

Index

⊒⊑ *Bradford Books*

William G. Lycan. LOGICAL FORM IN NATURAL LANGUAGE.

Gary Lynch, with commentaries by Gordon M. Shepherd, Ira B. Black, and Herbert P. Killackey. SYNAPSES, CIRCUITS, AND THE BEGINNINGS OF MEMORY.

Earl R. MacCormac. A COGNITIVE THEORY OF METAPHOR.

John Macnamara. NAMES FOR THINGS.

John Macnamara. A BORDER DISPUTE: THE PLACE OF LOGIC IN PSYCHOLOGY.

Charles E. Marks. COMMISSUROTOMY, CONSCIOUSNESS AND UNITY OF MIND.

Izchak Miller. HUSSERL, PERCEPTION, AND TEMPORAL AWARENESS.

Daniel N. Osherson, Michael Stob and Scott Weinstein. SYSTEMS THAT LEARN: AN INTRODUCTION TO LEARNING THEORY FOR COGNITIVE AND COMPUTER SCIENTISTS.

David Premack. "GAVAGAI!" OR THE FUTURE OF THE ANIMAL LANGUAGE CONTROVERSY.

Zenon W. Pylyshyn. COMPUTATION AND COGNITION.

W. V. Quine. THE TIME OF MY LIFE.

Irvin Rock. THE LOGIC OF PERCEPTION.

George D. Romanos. QUINE AND ANALYTIC PHILOSOPHY.

George Santayana. PERSONS AND PLACES.

Roger N. Shepard and Lynn A. Cooper. MENTAL IMAGES AND THEIR TRANSFORMATIONS.

Elliott Sober, editor. CONCEPTUAL ISSUES IN EVOLUTIONARY BIOLOGY.

Elliott Sober. THE NATURE OF SELECTION.

Robert C. Stalnaker. INQUIRY.

Stephen P. Stich. FROM FOLK PSYCHOLOGY TO COGNITIVE SCIENCE.

Joseph M. Tonkonogy. VASCULAR APHASIA.

Hao Wang. BEYOND ANALYTIC PHILOSOPHY.